YOU MAKE THE DIFFERENCE

THROUGH
EMPOWERING VOLUNTEER MANAGEMENT

Kay Kay

In collaboration with Tim Kay

You Make the Difference
www.youmakethedifference.net

Second Edition
First Edition published in 2012

Book designed and published by Tim Kay
University of Life

www.unioflife.net

You Make the Difference logo
© Tim Kay
All other illustrations and images © Microsoft Corporation

Author photo by Lina&Linda AB
Stockholm, Sweden

Copyright © 2013 Kay Kay
All rights reserved.
ISBN-10: 1483944573
ISBN-13: 978-1483944579

DEDICATION

For decades I have worked with wonderful volunteers whose dedication has been inspiring, and with people who have empowered, supported and manage volunteers with respect, and consideration. This book is dedicated to all of them with deep appreciation for the difference that they are making in the world

CONTENTS

ACKNOWLEDGMENTS

I am grateful for the ongoing collaborative support of Tim Kay and his skill in designing and turning my manuscript into books in various formats.

I appreciate Jane Cotton for her meticulous editing and for bringing her vast experience in the Voluntary and Community Sector to the improvement of this book.

I am grateful to Joan Wilmot for her supportive commenting upon the section on supervision.

I offer my appreciation to all the wonderful volunteers I have been privileged to work alongside whose dedication and commitment to their work has been inspiring. And to those who have managed these volunteers in an empowering and supportive manner with respect and consideration and from whom I have learned so much.

1

FINDING, ATTRACTING AND RECRUITING VOLUNTEERS

Introduction

The world is full of causes, problems and difficulties that require attention. The projects, groups and organizations dedicated to dealing with these are likely to become increasingly dependent upon volunteers in order to maintain their service and achieve their goals. Because of this the need for volunteer help could become greater than the supply available. This means that the ways of attracting, working with and keeping volunteers may require greater effort and closer attention than ever before.

There can be any number of reasons why people would choose a particular project, group or organization to volunteer with. It is up to groups and organizations to make themselves and their work as attractive to these people as possible, and, after recruiting them, to support them to be as effective as possible and to help them to find enjoyment and fulfillment through that volunteering.

In my experience, the most effective way of achieving this is through those volunteers feeling empowered in all of their volunteering activities. Anyone who has some responsibility for managing, directing or supporting volunteers would be wise to develop their skill for supporting the empowerment of those volunteers.

There is a belief that empowerment is not something that one person can provide for or develop in another and that empowerment is something that has to be self-generated in and by each individual. While this may be the case, there are unquestionably attitudes and behaviors that we can each develop that will support the self-empowerment of other people; just as there are attitudes and behavior that we can suppress in ourselves to prevent these from undermining other people.

Regardless of their reasons for volunteering these people ought to be highly respected and deeply appreciated. It is important to remember that they will be involved in volunteer activities through choice. They will be giving their time freely. They will be offering their skills, expertise and experience because they want to make a contribution. Without them many organizations and projects might not get off the ground, may not function well or fully achieve their purpose. In some cases, they might not continue to exist.

Finding your volunteers

Identifying your need for volunteers

Q

Questions to consider:
1. What volunteer roles need to be filled in your project, your group or your organization?
2. Who are the people you need?
3. How will you find them?

Identifying the roles

In any project, group or organization there are a number of obvious roles to be filled. Some of these will be management roles that will be similar in most situations. The roles involved in the provision of the service offered and the work being carried out by the group will of course vary.

In larger organizations management roles might be paid employment. In many small projects and groups most, often all, of the roles will be filled by volunteers.

It is worth remembering that there are likely to be any number of roles that are less obvious or may be seen to be nonessential in a project. Often, little attention is given to either identifying or filling these roles due to lack of funding, lack of awareness or lack of time and personnel.

Time spent on visioning the full potential of the project could increase awareness of the breadth of volunteering activities that could help the organization reach its potential.

Options to consider:

Go through all the activities carried out within and by your project, group or organization. Imagine how it could look in 5 years' time if it was to receive the appropriate volunteer support.

Break these activities into tasks. Note which large tasks volunteers could handle and which small tasks could be assembled into a role for a volunteer. This is an interesting exercise for a group to carry out because it can also identify the work actually being done, work that could be done and work that might currently be being done in an inefficient manner or which might not need to be done at all.

A Brainstorming session could also be a way to identify roles that might be filled by volunteers. As many people engaged in the project as possible ought to be involved in this process so that the widest variety of experience can be represented.

Make a list

Make a list of any of the roles and functions that could be carried out by volunteers in the future.

-

-

-

-

-

-

-

-

-

Finding the appropriate people to fill these roles

Ask around. The Voluntary and Community sector in most countries will be a network of networks containing people who are likely to know just the right individuals for any number of roles.

Some people with the skills needed might not be currently volunteering those skills. These people may be willing even eager to contribute some time to a project or cause that inspires them. They might only need to be asked.

Attracting the attention of volunteers

Q

Questions to consider:
   a.   Do people know that your project/group/organization exists?
   b.   Do they know what kind of work you do?
   c.   Do they know what volunteer opportunities are available within your organization?
   d.   How best could you get across to them who you are, what you do and what help you need with your work?
   e.   Are people aware of the benefits of working with you?

> In voluntary groups and organizations desperately trying to fulfill their commitments there may seem to be little time or resources spare for attracting the attention of potential volunteers. And yet, these are just the circumstances where more volunteer help is most often needed.

Options:
1. Design a strategy

Design a strategy for making sure that people know that your project, group or organization exists; what kind of work is being carried out and what volunteer roles are available within it.

You might consider seeking volunteer support for creating this strategy from a person with marketing experience.

2. Website

So much personal research is now done online. Even the smallest of charities and voluntary groups have websites. How attractive and effective is yours? Is it easy for people to navigate and find information about you and your volunteering opportunities?

3. Newsletter

Do you produce a newsletter? Whether this is posted on your website or mailed to your members and supporters it is a handy way of regularly bringing attention to your volunteering needs. Producing your newsletter could be a volunteer role, which in my experience is an interesting and inspiring voluntary activity.

4. Public lists

Lists of local groups and organizations are usually made available in libraries and other public places. Put up notices in all the places you can think of describing your group's aims and the skills and support you need to fulfill your objectives.

5. Local coordination

Many towns, rural and urban areas have a coordinating body that acts as a hub for sharing information and sometimes resources among local volunteer and community groups. Make sure that information about your work is well represented, current, is easily seen and accessible.

6. Voluntary Service Organizations

In many countries, Voluntary Service Organizations and similar bodies are a regional or international way of linking voluntary organizations and groups together and making known the work they do to a wider audience. There are often opportunities for posting notices on their websites or in their newsletters. Have pieces written for these about your current activities and mention your volunteering opportunities. The person writing these pieces could be a volunteer.

7. Presentations

Have people within your group ready, willing and able to make private and public presentations about your group and its activities. Create one or more specific power point presentation that anyone can easily offer. These people could be volunteers.

8. Speaking engagements

Have people within your organization accept or create invitations to speak to groups of people. Sometimes speaking engagements attract a fee or a donation from the audience, which could help to fund your work. Learning how to be an effective public speaker is a wonderful tool for self-development. Toastmasters, is an organization that offers supportive ways to develop this skill and, because it is a global network, opportunities exist within it to make contact with many like-minded people. People speaking about your work could be volunteers.

There are a number of other ways of finding volunteers:

a. In your emailing and conversation with people mention that you are looking for volunteers and ask them to spread the word.

b. Talk to people who you know are involved in volunteer work to see if they know of people who could be interested in volunteering with you. However, it is not supportive of other groups to poach their volunteers!

c. Have everyone in your organization ask their family, friends or colleagues if they know of people who could be interested in being involved in the good work you do.

d. Some areas have Volunteer Centers that register people wanting to volunteer. These act as agencies to place people in volunteering positions that are suited to their skills and experience and which they might enjoy.

Seeking advisers

Remember that Advisers can be volunteers too!

There is a lot of wisdom and experience going to waste out there. Through unemployment, redundancy, voluntary or enforced retirement, there are many people with valuable knowledge and experience who are no longer in a position to use them. These people, especially retirees, may not want to find replacement employment or to spend a lot of their newly acquired leisure time in a working environment. However, they may be willing to spend a small amount of time offering their knowledge and experience in an advisory capacity. This might also apply to people, who, through promotion or a change of career, are no longer using some of their specific skills and experience.

> Experts can advise on almost any subject: fundraising and financial systems; management strategies and service provision; IT systems, people management, interpersonal communications, meeting methods and many more areas that could be beneficial to organizations, groups and projects.

Ask around

Put the word out and ask around. People working in businesses or agencies might know of former colleagues now retired or moved on who might be willing and interested in being a volunteer adviser to your group.

Make a list

Make a list of new strategies that could help your organization to attract new volunteers.

-

-

-

-

-

-

-

-

-

-

-

-

-

-

-

-

-

-

Recruiting new volunteers

Q

Questions to consider:
1. Why would people choose your project/group/organization to volunteer with?
2. How can you help people to want to give their time, skills and experience to your group?
3. What might they need from you in order to say yes?
4. What can you offer potential volunteers?
5. How can you help them to make a firm commitment to your group and to the work that you do?

> Recruiting and enrolling new volunteers is likely to become on increasingly competitive business.

You may be required to put some thought and effort into encouraging people to choose to volunteer in your project, group or organization. They may need to see good reasons to want to give their time, skills and experience to your group rather than to another.

What can you offer to potential volunteers? In order to best answer this question it could first be useful to consider why people volunteer and what they might want to get out of their volunteering activities and experience.

Reasons for volunteering

There are many different reasons for volunteering, however, most people volunteer for reasons that fit into these main categories:

Caring

These would be caring people who want to help. Some people become volunteers in organizations when they, or the people they care about, need whatever it is that will be provided. People volunteer in projects and organizations that have helped them or someone close to them in the past. Some organizations have a reputation for care that inspires volunteers to join them.

"The capacity to care is what gives life its deepest significance."
Pablo Casals

Using skills

Some people are looking for ways to use their skills for the benefit of others. There are people who can see that their skills could be useful to individuals or organizations. They feel their skills could be more usefully employed than in only just their present circumstances. People might choose to volunteer in a project, a group or an organization where they see that their skills and experience would be most effective and maybe most appreciated.

Interest and Passions

Some people might want to do something worthwhile in the areas of their interests and passions. Many people volunteer their time to matters that interest them or who want to put their interests and passions to better use.

Self-improvement

Some people want to learn new skills, gain experience or build or rebuild their confidence. They may believe that some aspect of their present circumstances might be improved upon by opportunities available through volunteering.

Making contact

Some volunteers are seeking relief from isolation by making contact with others for companionship or friendship.

Using time

Those people with a lot of time on their hands such as retired, unemployed or young people during their gap year or their summer holidays, may want to do something interesting or useful with that time.

Fulfillment

Many people volunteer to have more meaning and purpose in their lives.

From my experience it seems that most people volunteer for a combination of these reasons.

It would be worth remembering that it is beneficial to consider that all of these reasons are valid and none of them are better than any other.

What might people want to receive from their volunteering?

In our working lives it is natural to want a job that is fulfilling and rewarding and not only in the monetary sense. It is natural to want to get some satisfaction from a job well done. It is natural to want to get a sense of achievement from our efforts and our creativity. So, why would our attitude to volunteering be any different? Why would we suppose that there is something wrong in wanting to receive some sense of satisfaction from our volunteer activities?

There seems to be a widely held belief that service ought to be its own reward and that it is better to give without any thought of receiving. I believe it is natural to want to get something out of putting in effort and contributing time, expertise and experience. It is quite reasonable for people to want to get some of their own needs met while they are meeting the needs of others through volunteering their valuable time, skills and experience.

Those who need support and who benefit from the volunteers input rarely mind what people's reasons are for volunteering. In my experience those people receiving support usually want their volunteer helpers to also benefit in some way from the efforts they make.

> There is now a better understanding that the world works best when it is in balance. In the world of volunteering, balance exists when there is a sense of giving and receiving, when win-win situations can be achieved.

As well as the satisfaction of a job well done and the feelings of accomplishment in knowing that they have made some positive difference, there may be wishes, wants and needs that people have, which could be met through volunteering with your project, your group or organization.

Options:
   a. Consider those wishes, wants and needs and find ways for your organization to meet as many of them as possible.
   b. Let potential volunteers know the ways in which volunteering with your project can provide opportunities for them to fulfill some of their wishes, wants and needs.

Fulfilling a wish to meet new people
From time to time people want or may feel the need to meet new people, to expand their current circle of friends or create a new one. This

may be brought about by some change in circumstances such as relocating, getting married or getting divorced, having babies or seeing grown-up children leaving home. The friends that people had before their circumstances changed may not be the ones they need or want afterwards.

> As we age or develop ourselves, our interests and the topics of our conversations may change. Changing opinion or attitude towards such things as politics or religion might create a need to find those who share our new thoughts and ideas.

Options:
1. Show that by joining your existing group, people could find a simple way of establishing a network of new friends after relocation.
2. Show that volunteering in your organization can offer opportunities to meet people who are in circumstances similar to the ones in which people now find themselves.
3. Show that through involving themselves in your project, people might find others who share their new interests or people quite different from those with whom they would normally associate.

What better way could there be to find compatible friends than through the activities that demonstrate the values that are held in common?

This seems to be a stronger basis for friendship than chance meetings in such venues as pubs or clubs.

Fulfilling a need for getting out and about
Sometimes people just need a reason to get out of the house. This may be as a result of living alone or perhaps when their house is packed to the rafters with family.

Being alone can become a difficult habit to break - even when people don't enjoy it. The longer they spend on their own the more difficult it can be for them to reach out to other people, to engage strangers in conversation, maybe even to pick up the phone or take that step out the front door.

> When a person's life is taken up with family matters he or she might crave conversation with people about things other than family issues or concerns.

Options:

    a.   Show that volunteering in your project could give people access to others who share their interests and with whom conversation about that common interest could flow easily.

    b.   Show that taking time out from family responsibilities, to pursue interests that do not include family, is not selfish.

    c.   Show that a short time each week doing something in your project that inspires and stimulates them, with people from outside their family circle, can be refreshing. People might return home feeling renewed by the confirmation that they are more than a parent, more than the carer of someone.

Fulfilling a wish to find new interests

For some people, their routine might be the same, day in, day out. They might do the same things at work every day, their conversations may be about the same topics; they might be lacking the spark of inspiration that spurs them to do something new.

Option:

    ➤   Show ways in which volunteering in your project could be interesting, even exciting, and which might broaden people's horizons and relieve the potential tedium of their everyday lives.

Fulfilling a wish to pursue old interests or passions

Sometimes people need a reason to resurrect something they used to enjoy or were passionate about.

It is worth remembering that to some people the amount of time and effort this might take may not seem justifiable if it is only for their own benefit or pleasure.

Options:

    a.   Show that through volunteering with your project there might be something people once had a passion for that they could now bring back into their life.

    b.   Show ways in which through your organization this renewed passion could benefit others.

Fulfilling a need to fill some gap

A change in circumstances can create gaps in people's lives that need to be filled. The loss of full-time employment as a result of retirement or redundancy can open up a yawning gap of unused days. The loss of a loved one due to bereavement or separation can leave behind a gap needing to be filled with some sort of activity. Grown up children leaving home can leave a huge gap in the lives of full time parents.

Options:
a. Show that volunteering with your group can be a productive and rewarding way for people to use newly released time.
b. Show that being of help to others through your project could provide them with the means to find some replacement for what has been lost or for something that is no longer easily accessible.

Fulfilling a need to gain experience
Some people need opportunities for work experience. Gaining experience from volunteer activities in their chosen profession or the kind of work that they will be applying for can greatly improve their employment chances.

Options:
a. If appropriate, show that opportunities for paid work might become available through the contacts made during a volunteering experience in your project.
b. Show that working as a volunteer with your organization might bring them into contact with people they would not normally meet in social circumstances or in their regular work environment. Show that the people they work alongside in a common cause might recognize their abilities and characteristics and may be in a position to offer to them, or recommend that they be offered, new or improved working opportunities.

Fulfilling a wish to learn or improve skills
Many people have a wish and sometimes a need to learn new skills or improve their current skills and abilities.

Options:
a. If appropriate, show that your organization offers skills training to volunteers.
b. Show how this creates the mutual benefit of people gaining more skills and the organization having another skilled volunteer available to it.
c. Show that even if your organization is unable to offer training, people can still improve their skills through volunteering with you.
d. Show how many of the people they volunteer with could have knowledge and experience about some subject that could be

handed on to them.

e. Show how being with these people, observing and the copying what they do and how they do it, could help people to become more skilled. Being in proximity to people doing things well can inspire them to reach a higher level of competency.

Fulfilling a desire to use time and skills productively

Not everyone has fascinating and rewarding paid employment. In some financial climates many people might be grateful for any job they can get.

> If daily work is repetitive, boring or unfulfilling, there may be the desire for people to use the skills they have to engage in other activities that could be meaningful.

Option:

> ➤ Show how through volunteering with you, people might be able to use their skills and some spare time in interesting and useful ways.

Fulfilling a need for personal development

Many individuals are now looking for ways in which to develop themselves as a person and through which they might improve their self-confidence.

> Volunteering can provide many opportunities for self-expansion and development that may not be easily available in paid employment.

Even thinking about volunteering might have already been supportive to a person's personal development.

Option:

> ➤ Show the kinds of opportunities for personal development that your project can offer to volunteers.

Fulfilling a wish to feel appreciated

It is important to remember that some people might receive very little appreciation in their day-to-day lives. In the workplace their endeavors may go unacknowledged and unappreciated. This may also be the case at home. In both places their efforts might go unnoticed or only noticed when they receive criticism or disapproval from others.

> Some people might interpret criticism of their efforts or their behavior as a disapproval of them as individuals, which can be very demoralizing.

Options:
- a. Show how the self-esteem and self-confidence of volunteers could be improved and enhanced by working in your organization where, rather than being judged or criticizing, their efforts could be received with gratitude and respect.
- b. Show how even the simplest of volunteer activities are often deeply appreciated by the people who benefit from them.

Fulfilling a need for a sense of purpose

> For most of us, a sense of purpose is what gets us springing out of bed in the morning. It is what keeps us going when things get tricky. It is what helps us overcome all sorts of obstacles.

Research indicates that having a sense of purpose is important for human beings. It has shown that having purpose can keep people alive in the most appalling situations and that having no sense of purpose can be life diminishing even in the most comfortable of circumstances.

It seems that depression and physical and emotional trauma can be more quickly overcome when the people experiencing them have a sense of purpose in their lives. Even when there are no major difficulties to overcome, our lives may seem colorless, meaningless even, if we are without purpose.

Loss of purpose sometimes comes along with other losses: loss of job, loss of relationship, loss of a loved one or a loss of faith.

Sometimes people lose their sense of purpose when they have achieved what they have set out to do. This could be anything from bringing up children safely to adulthood, reaching a position in an organization or paying off the mortgage. Or it may be a belief that life has passed them by and they might never achieve their dreams.

Options:
- a. Show that whether people are young and have not yet discovered

their sense of purpose; or older and have achieved one purpose and are looking for another; or if they have somehow lost their sense of purpose, then they might find or regain a sense of purpose through volunteering with your organization.

b. Show that your group has a purpose, an intention and a goal that is important and meaningful. Show that there are plenty of things within your project in need of some purposeful attention.

Fulfilling a desire to give back

People sometimes feel the need to give back or to show appreciation for the help and support they have received.

Losing a loved one to a terminal disease, a preventable accident or a destructive addiction can inspire people to be supportive in finding cures and in raising awareness about those issues.

Having overcome some major difficulty with the support and guidance of people who understood what they were going through can inspire people to also become one of those supportive people.

In these circumstances a desire to give back might be a strong force in a person's life. They may want to show gratitude and make a contribution through volunteering to organizations that have been supportive to them or to those they care about.

> Perhaps through being appreciative of what they have in their life, people might want to give something back into society through offering care, help and support to those less fortunate than themselves.

Option:

Show the many ways in which your organization can offer people opportunities to fulfill their wish to make some kind of repayment for help received or their desire to make a positive contribution towards creating solutions to the problems of society.

Make a list

Make a list of possible new strategies that could help your organization to recruit more volunteers.

-

-

-

-

-

-

-

-

-

-

-

-

-

-

-

-

-

-

-

-

-

-

Values and Ethics

When a group or organization is clear about its values and ethics it is likely to attract the volunteers who have those same values and ethics.

It is worth remembering that when an individual is looking for a group or an organization to volunteer with they will probably be looking for one that has the same ethics and values that they hold dear.

> If you have not fully established what your group's values and ethics are, it would be wise to do so before attempting to attract volunteers.

Responding to approaches

Any plans for recruitment ought to include a strategy for responding to approaches from potential volunteers.

If your group or project is small, then perhaps everyone involved in it could respond to approaches from potential volunteers. In this case all of the members of your group ought to have a clear idea of the work carried out by the group, what volunteer opportunities are available, the good reasons why people might consider volunteering with your project and what benefits this might offer.

It might however be more efficient to nominate one individual to be the contact person. As well as having all the above information at their fingertips, this person ought to be enthusiastic about the project and embody the values and ethics agreed upon by the group.

In larger organizations, one person or perhaps a team of people is likely to be appointed to the recruitment of volunteers. Their direct telephone number or e-mail address is probably the one that is made public. Obviously, if telephone communication is directed through a switchboard, the operators will need to know to whom to direct a potential volunteer. As these operators are often the first line of contact with the organization, they too ought to be well conversant with, and enthusiastic about, the work of the organization.

It is wise to bear in mind that your current volunteers are on the front line regarding recruitment. Potential volunteers are likely to ask them for information about your organization, especially about their experiences of a volunteering with you. Your volunteers ought to be fully aware of the aims and the activities of the organization, what the volunteering opportunities are within it and whom potential volunteers need to contact.

> Remember that overworked, undervalued and resentful volunteers are not good advertisements for your project and they are not likely to encourage others to join your group. Having volunteers who feel appreciated and fulfilled in their work with your organization might be your best method for recruiting others.

Getting to 'yes'

The recruitment stages covered so far have been what would mostly be considered to be 'marketing'. Now you have reached what could be called the 'sales' stage.

Once a potential volunteer has made contact with you, treat them as gold dust, just as you would a potential funder or valuable client. I have always believed that people are any organization's greatest resource. This is likely to become increasingly apparent with volunteers in the Voluntary and Community Sector over the coming years as available financial resources become more thinly spread or disappear altogether.

Option:

> Create handouts or e-mails about your group's successes, the work currently being undertaken, future or potential projects and the joys and benefits of volunteering with your organization. Make these as specific as possible for a variety of people's circumstances and interests and have them ready to be pulled from a file preferably after being topped and tailed specifically for each individual volunteer.

Have mechanisms in place for recording and making secure the details of everyone who approaches you regarding volunteering. Even if people are not willing or able to volunteer immediately, their circumstances might change in your favor in the future. Also, opportunities may open up in your organization that will be suitable for them and you might want to be able to contact them.

Make a list

Make a list of possible new strategies suitable for responding to approaches from potential volunteers.

-

-

-

-

-

-

-

-

-

-

-

-

-

-

-

-

-

Interviews

Have a clear procedure for discussions or interviews with potential volunteers. Treat potential voluntary members attending interviews with respect and courtesy. Be interested in them. Find out who they are, what inspires them to volunteer and what wishes or needs they would like to have met through their volunteering. Be enthusiastic and well informed about your organization and its work.

When the aims, values and benefits of your organization, group or project are compatible with the aims, values, wishes and needs of a potential volunteer, those people are likely to be inspired, even eager to join you.

Make that joining simple, easy and as immediate as you possibly can.

This is no time for vagueness, waffle or indecision on your part. As soon as they say 'Yes', take some of the following actions:

1. Sign them up.
2. Give them some token of their belonging to your group, such as a name badge or a letter of welcome.
3. If appropriate, show them around your facility.
4. Introduce them to the people who are now their colleagues.
5. If possible introduce them to or give them the details of their Mentor.
6. If possible, start them straight away on something or give them a clear start date and time.
7. At the very least give them some appropriate reading matter or training information to take away with them.
8. Make sure they are aware of your appreciation of their commitment of their time, skill and experience to your group. Project or organization.

A word of caution

> During the recruitment of volunteers when extolling the virtues and the quality of the benefits of your organization it is essential to be honest. Avoid offering misleading information or making claims that are untrue. Avoid making promises that cannot be kept.

2

SECURITY SCREENING

We would all like to trust that everyone who volunteers with any organization is doing so with a sincere desire to help out and give back, which for most people is the case. Unfortunately, as the old saying goes: 'it only takes one bad apple' to do harm to individuals and to the reputation and credibility of an organization.

> To prevent cases of misconduct or abuse, it is more important than ever to know who is involved in your organization, especially when children or vulnerable people are affected.

There have been reported many horror stories about strangers - or worse, people in trusted positions - who have harmed or abused children and elderly persons. Instances have been reported of convicted sex offenders seeking to volunteer with children's organizations.

Maintaining a safe environment as well as meeting increasingly tougher requirements by governments makes screening a necessity for today's modern voluntary and not-for-profit organizations. Conducting proper volunteer background checks can accomplish this.

It is worth remembering that with effective volunteer screening, organizations can be proactive in meeting legal requirements and ensuring that volunteers meet the organization's standards.

Legal requirement

Depending upon where in the world the volunteering takes place there is often no one law that says all volunteers must be checked. Rather, the rules that apply to volunteers can be as varied as the duties volunteers perform and the organizations they serve.

For example, countries may have laws that require background checks for employees and volunteers for activities the government regulates, such as schools and nursing homes. Quite likely, they will require some sort of screening for all volunteers who work for a government agency or state-funded facility, especially agencies that serve children, the elderly, or the disabled.

In the 21st Century, lawmakers have been steadily adopting new laws that either require or facilitate volunteer background screening. In some cases, new laws have been passed to strengthen existing, poorly crafted laws.

Some countries have introduced new schemes to replace and improve upon the old disclosure arrangements for people who work with vulnerable groups. In most cases these new schemes are intended to:

> ➤ Help to ensure that those who have regular contact with children and protected adults through volunteer work do not have a known history of harmful behavior.
> ➤ Be quick and easy to use.
> ➤ Reduce the need for people to complete a detailed application form every time a disclosure check is required.
> ➤ Strike a balance between proportionate protection and robust regulation.
> ➤ Make it easier for voluntary organizations to determine who needs to be checked to protect their client group.

Usually, legislation or recommendations call for some form of registration system for all those who work with children and vulnerable adults that would confirm that there is no known reason why an individual should not work with these client groups.

These requirements are intended to help local communities flourish and become stronger, safer places to live. They have mostly been built upon what has been learned from previous disclosure and disqualification services to develop efficient systems that will strengthen protection for vulnerable groups and reduce bureaucracy.

Even so, it seems that there has been much confusion over what was happening with new legislation and requirements - including within the departments charged with administering them. This has led to some insecurity amongst organizations, which has taken time to dispel.

In many cases a definite improvement is the clarity that individuals usually do not need to have (and pay for) a different disclosure for each voluntary/paid job they have and that there will be improved updating of information as the databases build up information.

Sensible precautions

In situations where background screening is not mandatory or a strict legal requirement, many volunteer organizations may still find background screening prudent. Like businesses, voluntary organizations must respond to the needs and fears of their clients.

> Parents have a legitimate right to assurance that their children are safe, whether at school or weekend soccer practice. Adult children of elderly parents will want to know their loved ones are not targets for abuse.

Failure to maintain trust can be devastating to an organization, leading to loss of community support, loss of funding, or even a lawsuit for negligent selection of a volunteer. When faced with an unfortunate incident involving a volunteer, an organization might fare better if they can show that they have made efforts to conduct an appropriate background check.

> The ultimate goal is to verify people's identity and weed out potential problems, especially problems that could arise from an undisclosed criminal history.

The kind of information gathered

It is up to each voluntary organization to honestly assess the need to gather information beyond a minimum criminal history check. The main consideration ought always to be the volunteer position to be filled and the background information needed for the organization to make a decision upon risk-based assessment that the volunteer is an appropriate candidate. Background screening is sometimes defined in its broadest sense as 'the overall collection, maintenance, retrieval and use of data about a person's background, from any source.'

The fact that information is readily available does not make the use of it necessary. The first step is to identify the volunteer's responsibilities and evaluate the risk associated with those duties. An organization is justified in checking the driving record of a volunteer who transports children to off-site activities. A credit check could be desirable for a volunteer who handles the organization's funds. In other circumstances there might be debate about whether a person's personal credit problems equate to a risk to an organization. Of limited value perhaps is use of a credit check as a character-assessment tool for jobs that do not involve handling money.

Remember: The most basic rule ought always be the collection of the minimum amount of information necessary to accomplish the purpose.

> Asking a volunteer to agree to an open-ended background check is precisely the kind of thing that sometimes prompts a negative reaction.

Furthermore, collection of only necessary data is in keeping with most established guidelines for data collection.

In the end, there really is no 'one-size-fits-all' background check.

Volunteer's objections to background checks

Some volunteers are deeply concerned about background checks. In some instances, long-time volunteers have resigned over an organization's newly instituted screening policy. New volunteer recruits may abandon their application rather than submit to screening.

> Privacy and security of personal information are common objections that volunteers have to background screening. Volunteers may also feel screening creates an atmosphere of distrust or suspicion.

However, when the past consequences of the absence of screening are considered, when people with predatory motives have had easy access to children and vulnerable people, the need for screening becomes obvious. With this understanding, most volunteers are willing to comply with regulations that apply to everyone in their situation.

What is involved?

Background screening involves gathering information about an individual. The process starts with the collection of personal data such as name, address, telephone number, present and past addresses, and Social

Security number. However, in these days of identity theft, it is common sense for people to wish to protect their personal information. Sharing personal data with anyone defies core advice for preventing identity theft and so data security is a major concern. Volunteers have a legitimate right to know that their personal information will be kept secure, either with online encryption systems or in locked filing cabinets.

Questions may also arise about the amount and kinds of information covered in any background check. Does the information to be collected relate to the job? For example, would an organization routinely ask its volunteers to agree to a credit check when the job does not require money handling?

Remember: Volunteers' concerns about data privacy and security can often be allayed if an organization provides a good written policy addressing privacy and data security issues.

The minimum privacy protection a volunteer can expect

Notice and consent are the cornerstones of privacy protection. Proper notice ought to include more than vague, all-inclusive statements about what the organization may collect. Instead, adequate notice would include a statement telling the volunteer:

a. The information that will be collected for the background screening.
b. How that information will be collected, e.g. through official government sources or a commercial screening company.
c. The name and contact information of that commercial screener.
d. Sources consulted for the screening.
e. The period of time encompassed by the screening.
f. Whether screening will be conducted once, annually, or on a continuing basis.
g. A statement of the consequences of declining to authorize screening.
h. A notice of additional rights.

Volunteers ought also to have:
➢ The first opportunity to review information, especially negative data.
➢ The right to appeal against disputed or inaccurate information.
➢ Assurance that personal data and information collected from the background screening will not be used for other purposes.
➢ Assurance that personal information will be securely stored, and access available only to those who have a need to know.

Finding a balance

In today's security-conscious climate, organizations are faced with a growing challenge - how to accomplish their mission while protecting the vulnerable population served. At the same time, organizations that rely on volunteers must perform a delicate balancing act - how to properly screen out bad apples without alienating dedicated, privacy-conscious volunteers.

Options for screening volunteers

There are several options. The choices depend largely on the volunteer job involved and the organization's policy as to what information is necessary to clear the candidate. A volunteer background check is likely to include a criminal history check.

1. To find out whether a potential volunteer has a criminal past, an organization may have direct access to government criminal history repositories. Organizations might also employ professional background screening companies.

2. Many commercial companies that perform employee screening have established separate programs specifically for voluntary and non-profit organizations seeking to check volunteers. Organizations may also find that commercial screeners are faster and cheaper than screening through state data repositories and might offer bulk rates or reduced fees for volunteer screening.

3. Professional screening companies may be found through recommendations from other voluntary and non-profit organizations. National organizations might contract with one company that performs screening for all their outlying posts. Check Web sites for Professional Background Screeners.

4. There is, in addition, a great deal of personal information available through the Internet. In some countries for example, Sex Offender registries are readily available on the Internet and some jurisdictions make criminal and civil court records available through the court's Web site.

The process

Organizations ought to first adopt written policies for screening volunteers as well as stated privacy and data security policies. Local organizations affiliated with a national organization will generally have guidance from their headquarters.

Volunteer screening policy

As a minimum, a volunteer screening policy would:

a. Clearly state the organization's position and practice for screening volunteers.

b. Identify the volunteer positions that require screening.
c. Identify the screening required for each volunteer position.
d. Identify the scope and sources for conducting background checks.
e. Identify the offenses or findings that would disqualify an applicant or current volunteer.
f. State the fees involved in screening and the responsibility of the volunteer for all or any portion of the fees.
g. Identify the frequency of background screening.

Privacy and data security policy

Suggested privacy principles to be included in an organization's policy:
➢ Openness with the volunteers.
➢ Purpose specification.
➢ Collection limitation.
➢ Use limitation.
➢ Quality.
➢ Security safeguards.
➢ Accountability

Policies ought to be posted on the organization's Web site or otherwise made easily available to all current and prospective volunteers. After determining the scope of the background check suitable for each volunteer position, organizations contact the appropriate authorities to find out whether their organization is eligible for access to this information. Then, if appropriate, the organization may conduct a check through official channels or a commercial screening company.

Commercial companies' privacy protections

In many parts of the world there are now reputable screening companies who follow recognized privacy standards when screening volunteers. Volunteers' rights regarding these ought to include:
a. Notice of and consent requested prior to the background check.
b. Notice of negative information before an adverse action is taken (such as refusing a volunteer's application).
c. A right to receive a copy of the report.
d. A right to appeal an adverse decision.
e. Proper disposal of any information included in a report.

In addition, any end-user of a report, e.g. a volunteer organization, must certify that the report will only be used for the purpose for which it was commissioned. In other words, an organization that gathers information for purposes of background screening will not then use that information to solicit donations, for example.

A reputable screening company would also:

> Provide necessary forms - either electronically or in paper format - for notice and consent as required by the regulating authority.

> Be well versed in various laws and be able to guide an organization through the screening process without running foul of state employment, consumer protection or discrimination laws.

> Companies can also help an organization navigate an appeal process in the case of inaccurate information.

Open-ended agreements are likely to draw a negative reaction from potential volunteers. Organizations faced with a broadly-worded consent form would be advised to work with their screening companies to develop a checklist that accurately identifies the information that will be obtained.

It is not foolproof

There is no foolproof 100% guarantee that any background screening will weed out all unsuitable candidates. There is even an argument that screening is unnecessary and creates a false sense of security. The argument goes that most people who commit a crime against a child, for example, are first time-offenders who could easily have cleared a prior background check. However, the requirement for volunteer screening, particularly for work with vulnerable people, is now firmly entrenched and expected to rise.

> If background screening protects the vulnerable amongst us and prevents future tragedies, surely it is worthwhile.

3

WORKING WITH VOLUNTEERS

When new volunteers join your ranks it is in your interest to look after them well and help them to be effective. That ought to be the responsibility of everyone in any organization or established group where one of the stated aims of the group would be that of mutual support. In larger organizations that responsibility might belong to the Volunteer Manager. Even so, everyone within that organization could be encouraged to be supportive towards new recruits.

Q

Questions to consider:
1. What makes a good volunteering experience?
2. How can you best use the volunteered skills that are offered to you?
3. What support do volunteers need to fulfill their roles effectively?
4. Which processes need to be in place for you to understand how effective, fulfilled and happy your volunteers feel?
5. What feedback systems need to be in place for volunteers to keep you informed of their progress, of their thoughts and feelings about their work and the organization and to offer suggestions for improvements?

What is a good voluntary experience?

To answer that question it could be useful to spend some time revisiting the previous section in this book on the wide range of reasons that people have for volunteering and what benefits people hope to receive from offering their gifts of time and skills.

> Having this understanding could guide you to create the circumstances and opportunities for people to have the sort of good volunteering experience they would wish for.

In interviews, conversations or group discussions within your organization these reasons and needs can be easily identified. While the expectations, attitudes and behavior of the volunteers are their responsibility, the people managing the project, group or organization have the responsibility for making the volunteering experience as good as possible.

Identifying the skills being offered

In any organization, particularly in small groups, it is vital that all of each volunteer's skills are recognized. These may become evident in interviews, conversations and group discussions, however, it is sometimes the case that a person will take on a role because it needs to be filled, while other skills and abilities, which might be even more valuable, may remain undetected.

> During recruitment, full attention ought to be paid to finding out the extent of the skills of potential volunteers; otherwise they may be placed as round pegs in square holes or underused by your organization.

Offering your volunteers the opportunity to engage in the process of identifying their Unique Combination of skills, interests, experience and available time that are described in ENJOYABLE AND VALUABLE VOLUNTEERING in the YOU MAKE THE DIFFERENCE series, could be of benefit. This book is available in paperback and e-book format from Amazon and is accessible through our website: www.youmakethedifference.net.

Using skills effectively

Having identified all the skills and talents and experience available to you, make sure that these are put to the most effective use. I have experience of volunteers with a set of skills perfect for one specific role being persuaded to fill a gap where quite other skills are required. This has led to unsatisfactory work and dissatisfied volunteers.

Remember: If a volunteer is willing to work in an area that does not best utilize their skills, make sure that is as temporary as possible while a better fit is explored. If a volunteer is willing to work in an area that requires some skills they do not possess, offer every opportunity for them to learn those necessary skills.

Beware of overloading volunteers

There might be an understandable temptation to ask volunteers working in one area to also assist in another area where help is needed or to do extra work when personnel are in short supply.

> Beware of overloading willing volunteers. This could be the quickest way to lose them!

People just joining a group will want to be accepted and so may feel obliged to do what is necessary in order to fit in. If a volunteer becomes overstretched this may lead to their burnout. That is unhealthy for them and may result in the group no longer having the support of that person.

While it is, of course, the responsibility of volunteers to take care of their own health and well-being, it is the responsibility of the people supporting or managing them to ensure that appropriate talents are fitted to tasks, that the time available for activities is realistically assessed and that the willingness and caring attitudes of volunteers are not exploited or abused.

Integrating volunteers

I have observed many occasions when newly recruited volunteers have been expected to find their own way through a maze of unfamiliar systems and procedures. It is sensible and efficient to have some mechanisms in place to help volunteers integrate into your organization.

Options:
a. Provide orientation programs aimed at showing new volunteers the ropes. Such programs ought to include familiarizing them with any systems and protocols that are in place.
b. Give training in any functions that volunteers will be expected to carry out, especially if these are likely to be unfamiliar to them or if they are specific to your project. In some circumstances these might be effectively conveyed in a short training manual or at the

very least in fact sheets.
c. Provide volunteers with Mentors. Mentoring is a simple and effective way of supporting new volunteers to learn about the project, how the systems work and what is required of them.

There are so many benefits to mentoring
1. New recruits can be smoothly integrated into the organization.
2. Being introduced to others by their Mentor can be a quick way for new people to learn who is who and to be more easily accepted by members of an established group.
3. Having an experienced and knowledgeable person available to them will help new people to quickly learn what is required of them.
4. Having someone to turn to with questions or concerns can prevent mistakes being made due to lack of experience.
5. Having a Mentor can prevent newcomers from feeling awkward or isolated.

Supporting volunteers to fulfill their roles effectively
Volunteers are usually most effective when:
➤ They know what they're supposed to do.
➤ They understand why they are supposed to do it in a particular way.
➤ They know when they are supposed to do it.
➤ They feel competent and confident in carrying out what is required of them.

Remember: Volunteers are likely to be less than effective if any of these four elements are missing. When these are absent it is usually as a result of inadequate training and/or poor communication.

Options:
a. Regularly check out that these elements are clearly communicated and fully understood.
b. Regularly check that volunteers feel competent and confident to carry out their tasks.
c. Provide easy ways for your volunteers to raise questions or concerns regarding any of these elements.
d. Have systems in place for responding immediately and respectfully to any of your volunteer's questions.

Make a note

Make a note of the procedures that can be put in place that will help volunteers to be quickly integrated and effective in your organization.

-

-

-

-

-

-

-

-

-

-

-

-

-

-

-

-

-

Agreeing values, ethics and conduct

> Establishing some values, ethics and conduct that everyone within your group/organization/project can agree to will provide a foundation upon which to build good working relationships and will go a long way towards guaranteeing sustainability.

If, at the start of a group coming together, processes are gone through that identifies the group's values and ethics, this will go a long way towards bringing inclusion and cohesion to the group.

> It is never too late for an established group to form an agreement about their shared values and ethics.

It is beneficial to discover the common ground or the differences between members of your group. People will have different priorities or personal agendas, which will influence or be influenced by their personal values and ethics. If people have been drawn together there is most likely to be enough similar threads of values and ethics among them that can be woven into an agreement to build the foundations of their work and to hold them together.

Although there will be specific values and ethics required for each project to effectively achieve its aims, there are a number of things that would be beneficial in those of any group:

- ➢ Respect,
- ➢ Honesty,
- ➢ Clarity,
- ➢ Straightforwardness,
- ➢ Responsibility,
- ➢ Tolerance,
- ➢ Cooperation
- ➢ Willingness.

Remember: When these eight words underpin the attitudes, communication, behavior and actions of individuals and the group as a whole that group is unlikely to go far wrong.

Common Ground Agreements

When the values and ethics of the group or organization are identified and decided upon by everyone involved, these could form the basis of a Mutual Agreement.

Whether called agreement, intention, commitment, statement of common ground or anything else, this can be a great aid to maintaining cohesion, congruency and trust within a group or organization. A wise group will produce an agreement or statement of common ground based upon these values and ethics for all new volunteers to sign.

The following example of a mutual group agreement has been adapted from the Statement of Common Ground devised many years ago in the Findhorn Community. This has proven to be a useful template for similar mutual agreements created by many groups and organizations around the world.

Mutual Agreement

1. Support

I wholeheartedly support the aims of this group and the wellbeing and ongoing development of all group members.

2. Personal integrity and respect

I will maintain high standards of personal integrity, embodying congruence of thought, word and action. I will respect other people, their views, origins, backgrounds, issues and experiences.

3. Direct communication

I will use clear and honest communication with straightforwardness, attentive listening and respectful responses. In public and in private I will avoid speaking in any way that maligns or demeans others. I will talk **to** people rather than **about** them and will not seek to gossip or collude. I will challenge any actions, manipulation or intimidation that I feel may be detrimental to myself or to others.

4. Responsibility

I will take full responsibility for my thoughts, words and actions. I am willing to listen to constructive criticism and to offer constructive feedback to others in a caring and appropriate fashion that will support each to grow. I acknowledge that there may be wider perspectives than my own and deeper concerns than those that immediately affect me. I will take responsibility to work through or put aside my personal issues for the benefit of the whole group.

5. Conflict resolution

I will make every effort to resolve all personal and group conflict as soon as possible. In the event of a dispute continuing unresolved I will adhere to the group grievance procedure or I may call for a friend, an independent observer or mediator to support a mediated process.

6. Cooperation

I will work cooperatively within the group and consider other people's views carefully and respectfully. I recognize that others may make decisions that affect me and I agree to respect the care, integrity and wisdom that they have put into the decision-making process.

7. Commitment

I commit to keeping these agreements and to exercising the spirit of this statement in all my dealings.

Signature

Date

The key words and phrases in an agreement can be put together in a similar short statement that can be made available to all interested people. This might take the form of a Statement of Values and Ethics, a Mission Statement or some similar statement of intent. It can be made evident in your literature and on your website.

Make a note

Make a note of what you would want to be included in agreements to be made among your staff and volunteer colleagues.

-

-

-

-

-

-

-

-

-

-

-

-

-

-

-

-

-

-

-

-

-

-

Challenging any broken agreements

When a group has created a statement of values and ethics that each member has agreed or committed to, then anyone in the group will be in a position to challenge any other member whose behavior demonstrates a disregard for those values and ethics.

Remember: The challenging of a person regarding their agreement can be more effective than directly challenging their behavior and certainly more supportive than making criticisms or judgments.

Q

'How does this help?'

This is a useful question to ask a group member whose behavior is outside the agreed parameters of the group's values and ethics. You could supportively challenge the person by saying something like: 'I notice the way you have been speaking to people does not seem to fit with your agreement to be respectful in your communications? Is there another way for you to say what you want to tell people and still keep to your agreements?'

Training volunteers

This is an area that is often woefully lacking in smaller organizations (and in some larger ones too!).

Necessary training

Training in the skills required and the systems used ought to be available to all volunteers. This will ensure that they are fully aware of what is expected of them and how to carry out the tasks in the way that the organization has found to be most effective. Without this, volunteers might not be as useful as they could be and organizations may find that they need more volunteers to do the work than is necessary.

Lack of training can lead to a high turnover of frustrated volunteers.

Personal development training

There are other forms of training that are rarely provided in most small and some large organizations that could be offered as a way of appreciating volunteers. These types of training could be described as Personal Development.

Many subjects can fit under this heading, such as interpersonal communications, time management, meeting skills etc. They are sometimes referred to as 'soft skills'.

In my experience, training in these skills for employees and especially for volunteers, is likely to be the first to be axed when finances become tight. So, how is it I am recommending these as rewards for volunteers? Because anything that can improve volunteers' confidence, develop their people skills or increase their awareness can also be of tremendous benefit to the organization. And, many organizations might not have to pay for it!

Option:

> Occasionally, odd pockets of small amounts of funding can be found to provide training in these 'soft skills', particularly for volunteers who are carrying out face-to-face activities with clients, especially when those clients are among the young, the aged or the vulnerable in society.

A group receiving such funding could offer to include in these training programs representatives of other local voluntary groups who would then be able to share the skills that they learn with their colleagues. Along with my partners and colleagues, I have encouraged the widening of the participation in our training programs in this manner whenever it has been possible.

In many groups and organizations there is rarely a budget for training, so other options for providing training need to be explored. In my experience there are a couple of ways in which training workshops can be made freely available to volunteers.

1. I have been happy to volunteer to run workshops on communication skills and meeting management in voluntary organizations around the world. I am certain that there are many other trainers and workshop leaders who would be willing to offer their skills as their donation to organizations they wish to support.

2. A few small groups could be gathered together for a training workshop with a volunteer trainer. Or as previously mentioned, representatives of many groups and organizations could be invited to a freely offered training workshop. These people could share their new skills and information with their fellow volunteers in their organizations.

Training expenses

Even in freely offered workshops, some expenses might be incurred for such things as materials, the production of handouts and for venue hire.

In my experience, most organizations can find a small amount in their budgets to donate towards the covering of these expenses and many volunteers are themselves willing to pay a small amount or offer a donation towards covering such expenses if the training is free.

I have found that people can be very creative in covering these expenses. For example, in a training of volunteers representing several organizations, one of those organizations could offer space in their building as the venue. Another could handle the photocopy of handouts etc. and other organizations might provide transport or the materials and equipment to be used.

When refreshments are required, especially if lunch is necessary, then participants could bring food to share. This can increase cooperation and help build or enhance relationships between participants.

> It is worth bearing in mind that most workshops and training programs carried out in groups are also excellent ways of building trust and developing cooperation.

Make a list

Make a list of more training opportunities that could be provided for your volunteers.

-

-

-

-

-

-

-

-

-

-

-

-

-

-

-

-

-

-

-

-

-

-

-

-

-

Trust and responsibility

Trust is built on mutual respect and high regard, a willingness and ability to cooperate and upon an absence of attitudes of blaming and shaming.

Trust, or lack of it, will develop in a group naturally over time. However, in my experience the more attention that is paid to consciously developing trust, the quicker trust will be established and the less likelihood there will be for much, if any, mistrust to form.

At the start of a project or when a number of new volunteers have joined a group it can be very beneficial to devote some time specifically to the development of group trust.

Group games

An enjoyable way of doing this is through playing group games together that have been specifically designed to develop trust amongst the members of a team or a group.

While there may be some friendly rivalry encouraged between teams in a few of these games, most provide opportunities for people in the groups to quickly develop trust in one another through activities that are fun and maybe even a little bit silly.

Sharing laughter and silliness has been shown to quickly and effectively dissolve barriers between strangers or between established group members and newcomers.

Remember: Some aspects of volunteer work can be, and sometimes need to be, serious; so providing volunteers with any opportunity to have fun can be extremely beneficial.

There may be people within your organization who could provide this opportunity or you could seek out facilitators skilled in this sort of activity. If they support the aims of your group they may be willing to offer a session as their donation to your project.

There are many examples of these types of games in the book ENJOYABLE & EFFECTIVE MEETINGS in paperback and e-book formats that are available from Amazon and accessible through our website. These are also available in the GUIDE TO GROUP GAMES, which is FREE to download from our website:
www.youmakethedifference.net/free-guides.

Building a culture of trust

Volunteers who are offering their time, skills and expertise in support of the group and for the benefit of others thrive on encouragement and mutual respect. When people feel recognized for their abilities and trusted to use those abilities responsibly they are more likely to do so than when feeling doubted or distrusted.

> Building a culture of trust depends upon people actually being trusted! Trust builds trust.

Trusting people to do things can build their confidence and by their taking of responsibility for their actions and behavior they demonstrate that they can be trusted.

When giving volunteers responsibility it is important that they fully understand what is expected of them and have everything they need to carry out that responsibility. That includes the belief that they are trusted. When giving responsibility to people, do so with confidence and show them that confidence. If people get a sense that they are not really trusted or that others have concerns that they might fail, this could undermine their self-confidence and actually bring about that failure.

When a volunteer makes a mistake it is advisable to include them in sorting it out. This is not intended to reprimand or embarrass them. It is done to help them to learn from the experience and to understand and take responsibility for the consequences of their actions. This can be done with compassion and support through constructive feedback.

Remember: Groups are less likely to be effective when attitudes of criticism and disrespect lead to feelings of disempowerment among the group members. This also applies to attitude. Negative attitudes can be harmful to the survival of a group or project.

Negative attitudes could include:

➢ Defeatism
➢ Cynicism
➢ Aggression
➢ Disempowerment
➢ Victimhood
➢ Undermining
➢ Sabotaging
➢ Blaming

> ➤ Shaming
> ➤ The seeking of scapegoats.

Positive attitudes that would be helpful in all group situations are:
> ➤ Cooperation
> ➤ Encouragement
> ➤ Open-mindedness
> ➤ Mutual support
> ➤ Mutual respect
> ➤ The recognition of opportunities
> ➤ Honest and direct communication
> ➤ Compassion
> ➤ Acceptance of people as they are

Make a note

Make a note of the ways in which trust could be increased within your project, group or organization.

-

-

-

-

-

-

-

-

-

-

-

4

CONSTRUCTIVE COMMUNICATION

An important foundation stone upon which trust and good working relationships develop is the way in which people converse with one another.

Communication that is empowering and supportive is Constructive Communication.

Constructive Listening

Q

A useful question to consider is:

How constructive is the listening within your organization?

People are listening constructively when they show that their intention is to listen and understand. There are a number of ways they can do this:

1. They stop what they are doing and give their undivided attention to the person who is speaking.
2. They allow enough time for the person to whom they are listening to satisfactorily complete their conversation.
3. They choose suitable settings in which they can hear clearly.

4. They encourage people to fully express themselves.
5. They listen with compassion and an open heart and mind: without interruption, judgment or criticism.
6. They avoid the temptation to give advice or fix people's difficulties before people have had a chance to work things out for themselves.
7. They clarify anything they don't understand and check out that what they heard was what was actually said or meant.
8. They make sure that those they have listened to have said everything they needed to say, and have felt accurately heard and fully understood.

Constructive Speaking

Q

How constructively do people in your group speak to one another?

This means speaking respectfully, clearly, directly, honestly, compassionately and supportively. People can do this by:

a. Speaking respectfully to all people at all times.
b. Saying what they mean and meaning what they say.
c. Clearly stating their ideas, suggestions, opinions and conclusions.
d. Honestly expressing how they feel about any situation.
e. Avoiding leaving things out, covering up emotions, pretending all is well or denying what it is they want or need.
f. Giving supportive feedback about what they observe or experience.
g. Speaking kindly and avoiding gossip.
h. Being compassionate by avoiding making judgments.
i. Avoiding making criticisms unless they are constructive and supportive.

If there is very little of this kind of communication going on and people are abrasive, disrespectful or even rude to one another, this is almost certain to result in disharmony within any group, which might lead to the ultimate ineffectiveness of any project.

> You can make the difference to your project/group/organization by modeling Constructive Communication at all times. You can have a strong, positive influence upon the communication within the group culture by encouraging the Constructive Communication of your colleagues.

Self-disclosure

The times when new volunteers join the organization can be used to consciously engage the group in some trust development. During some of the preliminary meetings, especially during the first one, time could be spent on people introducing themselves to one another in some depth and detail.

An aspect of building trust through communication is that of self-disclosure. This is when people talk openly about themselves, what's going on for them and how they are thinking and feeling. Unfortunately, this can be rare, even frowned upon or discouraged in some places.

> Trust is commonly greater in groups where people know a lot about one another, either because of their shared history or because of information learned through their mutual self-disclosure.

To some people, self-disclosure might be okay within families or between close friends, however, it might feel uncomfortable or threatening for them within a group of relative strangers. This can create a Catch-22 situation where people don't feel safe enough to talk about themselves and what they're really thinking or feeling because there is not enough trust in the group. And yet, there isn't enough trust in the group because people are not being honest and open about their thoughts and feelings.

Obviously, when talking about yourself, your concerns, your ideas, your thoughts and your feelings within a group, or anywhere else for that matter, it is important to use 'I statements': 'I notice... I think... I feel... I wonder... I have concerns about... I am alarmed to hear... I feel it might be better if we... I would like... I need to... etc., are suggestions of effective ways to start a sentence of self-disclosure.

You can make the difference in your project/group/organization by gradually and carefully becoming increasingly self-disclosing. This can be a powerful tool for creating a change in attitude towards speaking openly. I have observed immense relief being experienced by people in groups who realize this gives them permission and opportunity to speak honestly.

Self-disclosure can also be introduced among group members by gently encouraging more of it in informal conversations, group discussions and in meetings.

If there is a strong culture of people being aloof with one another and keeping themselves to themselves within the organization then the concept of self-disclosure will need to be introduced with compassion and sensitivity. This could prove to be well worth the effort when openness and honest communication begins to underpin trust in your organization.

In addition to self-disclosure, attention could be paid to eradicating blaming and shaming language within the organization.

Remember: When people develop the skill of talking about a situation without attempting to shift the blame away from themselves or apportioning blame to others the more opportunity there will be for trust to develop.

> When things can be discussed openly, without any attempt to shame or embarrass the people involved, the greater the likelihood there will be for trust to grow.

Giving instructions

Constructive Communication is a firm foundation for the delivery of instructions or directions to volunteers. It is vital that the person delivering instructions knows exactly what these are intended to achieve.

For instructions to be fully effective they need to be delivered in a way that those receiving them can easily hear and understand. They are most effective when given to the people who have the appropriate skills and experience and who have a sufficient amount of time available to carry them out. Volunteer time is often wasted or not fully utilized because the people in charge of a project or a task have given insufficient thought to how best to use that time. This is inefficient and wasteful of resources. It also shows disrespect to those volunteers who gift their precious spare time for the benefit of others.

> To ensure that the instructions have been heard accurately a useful habit to develop within the culture of the project, group or organization is that of requiring instructions to be repeated back by the person receiving them to the person delivering them.

Whilst this may seem a little contrived, odd or even silly to some people, my experience is that this can save a great deal of time, effort and money.

You can make a difference to your project, group or organization by requesting your instructions to be repeated back to you. Saying something like 'to make sure that I have included everything, please will you repeat back to me what you heard me say?'

You can also model this behavior by always repeating back any instructions that have been given to you. 'Let me check that I've got everything…' 'I want to make sure that I haven't missed anything…' 'I believe I heard you say…'

> If there is any doubt that some people within the organization might not be able to deliver instructions accurately, clearly and concisely, then it could be wise to create simple instruction sheets for some tasks.

This could be helpful to newcomers and would be a sensible thing to do if there is a high turnover of volunteers.

Giving and receiving feedback

Methods for giving and receiving feedback are now becoming standard practices in many groups and organizations in the private, public and third sectors.

Receiving feedback

Q

Useful questions to consider:
1. How will you know if a new system has been fully understood and is working well?
2. How will you discover how effective some training has been?
3. By what means will you learn how committed and content your volunteers are?

There are two ways to achieve this: direct and indirect feedback.

Indirect feedback

This is delivered gradually over time as systems fail, people don't do their work effectively, there is discontent and disharmony within the organization and people leave.

This kind of feedback is inevitable if the people who are organizing systems and managing people do so using the Ostrich method. This method is where they metaphorically stick their heads in the sand and wait for things to sort themselves out and hope that problems will go away. This managerial method is often based upon the vain hope of avoiding criticism and conflict or facing problems that might be difficult to deal with. There are a lot of Ostriches out there!

> By putting off or avoiding dealing with difficulties or in not setting up simple means for volunteers to offer direct and regular feedback, these people can create the very situations they are trying to avoid.

Direct feedback

Direct feedback is when volunteers are able to talk about progress, of how things are working, or not, and what they are thinking and feeling about things directly to the people who can do something about the situation.

In large organizations one-on-one conversations might not always be achievable. I this case, some other method for feedback to be given as directly as possible will need to be implemented.

Options for soliciting feedback

a. Ask for feedback from people who have received the service that is offered and from colleagues and volunteers at the completion of a procedure or an event. Let people know that the information about their experience is vital to the improvement and sustainability of the organization.

b. An opportunity for direct feedback might be made at the end of meetings and training programs and at intervals during the early stages of the implementation of new systems and procedures.

c. Regular feedback on the feelings, thoughts and attitudes of volunteers could easily be received during support meetings or come out of the meetings of Mutual Support Groups, (see later).

d. Small-group or departmental discussions would give people opportunities to offer feedback on how things are for them in their work. Their representatives could feed this information back to those at higher managerial levels.

e. Feedback forms could be created and made readily available and easily accessible to everyone within an organization and those served by it. These need to be created in such a way that any subject could be covered. While some tick boxes make for efficient form filling, care needs to be taken to not limit options or to restrict people on what they might want to feedback.

Using the feedback given

I once observed someone at the end of a session collect the feedback forms left by participants and dump them straight into the waste paper bin!

It is pointless asking for and receiving feedback if there is no intention of doing anything with it.

In fact, it's worse than pointless; it's wasteful, expensive and disrespectful.

Not only is it a waste of time and resources, it is a waste of valuable information. If people have taken the time and trouble to offer feedback they are likely to be paying attention to how that feedback is used. If volunteers already have concerns about a situation they may become disillusioned with the organization if they feel that their feedback has been ignored. Disillusioned volunteers are likely to leave and seek other groups or organizations to which they can offer their valuable time, skills and experience.

Complaints

Many people fear complaints because they think they are indications of failure. And yet, in most cases, complaints are valuable feedback.

Claire

A few years ago I was conducting a session with Claire, a manager in a voluntary organization to whom I offered voluntary coaching support.

Claire was upset because she had received some complaints about a system she had initiated. One complaint was from a member of the full-time staff, one was from a volunteer and another was from a client in receipt of the assistance offered by the organization.

I remembered a previous session in which Claire had not been prepared to consider the option of discussing this new procedure with her colleagues, volunteers or clients before implementing it. Now, I gently asked how she was going to handle this clear feedback. She protested that it was not useful feedback because only three people had responded in this way and nobody else had said anything.

We considered how difficult it could be to interpret the absence of feedback – which is of course a form of feedback – because it could mean so many things.

It might mean that the majority of people were happy with the situation and saw no reason to offer feedback. It could mean that people were indifferent to the situation and had no inclination to offer feedback. It may mean there was no easy way for them to offer feedback or even realize that it might be required or expected of them. It might mean that people had concerns about how any seemingly negative feedback might be received.

Claire said that she thought these three who had complained were horrible people and wondered why everybody couldn't just be nice.

I suggested to her that these three people might have been more helpful to her organization than all the other silent 'nice' people put together. I floated the idea to her that 'nice' people may not be the most reliable when it comes to honest feedback for a number of reasons:

1. Nice people usually don't like to make a fuss.
2. Nice people habitually avoid confrontation.
3. Nice people seldom give honest feedback if it's likely to make them or other people feel embarrassed or uncomfortable.
4. Nice people often keep their concerns and complaints from those individuals or organizations with whom they are unhappy.
5. Nice people rarely keep their thoughts about their dissatisfaction to themselves when talking with other people.
6. Nice people will usually tell their friends, family members and their colleagues about their concerns, especially if they feel by doing so they could prevent others from experiencing what they had gone through.
7. Nice people will give details and express their opinions about their concerns in a way that might be mistaken for facts.
8. If these nice people are sufficiently upset about something they are likely to go on and on about it, telling anybody who will listen.

> Nice people are an organization's worst public relations nightmare because they may be tearing the reputation of that organization to shreds without the organization having any idea about what is going on.

There may be no opportunity to hear about a problem, to work out the cause of it or to do anything to remedy it until it is too late.

People who complain are offering very clear feedback about something they are unhappy with. Complaints are opportunities rather than problems, unless they are unheard, ignored or not remedied.

Astute business leaders already know this. Many organizations, especially those in the retail business, have a complaints procedure under the heading of customer service. In the better ones, customers feel attentively heard, come to believe that their situation is fully understood with the result that the cause for their complaint quickly remedied. This process has allowed organizations to be alerted to potential faults, to put procedures in place to prevent them from being repeated and to build stronger relationship with their customers.

Obviously, it would be better if there is no cause for complaint in the first place and of course there are people for who complaining is a way of life. Even so, there is maturity and wisdom in seeing complaints as opportunities to improve working practices and offer better service.

> You could make the difference by helping your volunteers to turn any of their complaints into direct feedback that can be clearly received and appropriately acted upon.

Giving feedback

Feedback given to volunteers might be to appreciate them for what they are doing or to praise or complement them on work well done. Offering appreciative feedback will be covered in the next section.

Feedback may of course also be to express concern about volunteer's actions or behavior, to tell them that they have made an error or to explain to them how something needs to be done differently.

The trouble is that many people have difficulty in expressing themselves and delivering this kind of feedback. They might feel awkward, embarrassed or do not want to risk upsetting people. So, they either avoid saying anything and so give no feedback at all, in which case nobody learns and the situation is likely to worsen; or they deliver the feedback harshly, as criticism or judgment, and in a manner that can be demoralizing and disempowering for the recipient.

> Clear, honest, direct feedback does not need to be delivered in a critical or judgmental manner. It can easily be delivered with understanding, kindness and compassion.

Supporting people to improve

People make mistakes. They might not carry out instructions accurately. They don't always behave in the most appropriate manner. The whole point of feedback is to help people to improve, to develop, to grow. People can change their behavior and learn to do things better or differently. All they usually need is to be told in a way that they can hear and understand without feeling wrong, bad, stupid, hurt or rejected.

It is important to remember when delivering feedback that even when you are making a great effort to do so supportively, you are likely to be challenging someone's actions, behavior or methods of communication.

Hearing this can be uncomfortable for people, especially if they are not used to being challenged. Some people overreact or react very strongly to any form of criticism, real or imagined.

Creating a feedback sandwich

Feedback that might be uncomfortable for someone to hear could best be delivered between two slices of appreciation, encouragement or praise:

'I'm grateful to you for alerting me about this situation. However, I believe that it is part of your role and your responsibility to find a solution to this difficulty. I have every confidence in your abilities to sort this out.'

'I appreciate you for wanting to complete this so quickly. However, I am concerned that the finished result looks patchy. Please give it another coat; I feel sure you will be more pleased with the result. Thank you for your willingness to help us with this work.'

Imagine this Scenario:

A young volunteer has spent hours photocopying hundreds of copies of a report. Each sheet of paper has been photocopied on one side only. Here are some typical responses that might have been made to this volunteer. (These are based upon responses to similar situations that I have witnessed or heard about).

    a.   'You stupid girl, you've only copied on one side.'

    b.   'Who on earth told you to photocopy on one side only?'

    c.   'You've only copied on one side; have you any idea how much paper costs these days?'

    d.   'Anyone with half a brain would realize that a long report like this should be copied double-sided.'

    e.   'Yes, well, thanks for doing this. Pity you didn't think to photocopy it double-sided.'

    f.   No direct feedback is given to the volunteer only a sarcastic remark about 'paper not growing on trees!'

    g.   No direct feedback is given to the volunteer although the manager is in a bad mood for the rest of the afternoon.

    h.   Nothing is said to that volunteer who is never given photocopying to do in the future and does not know why.

These types of responses are either directly aggressive or made for the benefit of the person delivering them. When no direct response is made or a person is discounted or ignored, that is a passive form of aggression.

Often, someone's intention when delivering aggressive kinds of feedback is to vent their anger or to relieve their frustration. It might be to seek revenge on that person or to make himself or herself feel better through embarrassing or humiliating that person.

It seems to me that there is no need for this kind of feedback (which I suggest would fit under the heading of destructive communication). In my experience, this kind of feedback is rarely beneficial to anyone and often damages the relationship between the two people involved and undermines the self-esteem of the person receiving the feedback.

I believe there is always a way to deliver feedback constructively, even when people have made errors or their behavior, communication or actions have been inappropriate or have created problems.

> Feedback that is constructive contains a clear statement of the situation, a description of how the person giving the feedback thinks and feels about it and a request or a suggestion for that kind of situation to be handled differently in the future. This is what I call a complete feedback message.

Complete Feedback Messages

When offering this type of feedback we include these four elements: What we see, what we think, what we feel and what we need, would wish or would prefer to happen next or in the future.

It is useful to remember that all relationships thrive on complete messages. People can't know the true reality of a situation unless we share all our experience of it. It means giving accurate feedback about what we observe and clearly stating our thoughts and conclusions. It means saying how we feel, what we need and making straightforward requests or suggestions if we see possibilities for improvement or change.

Leaving any of these out of a feedback message can create confusion and distrust. People could be antagonized or turned off when they hear judgments. They are likely to be defensive when they feel they are being criticized or interrogated. They may be suspicious of conclusions arrived at that are not supported by observations.

> People who are defensive, angry, suspicious or turned off, are unlikely to clearly hear and accept the feedback they are given.

Creating Complete Feedback Messages

The idea of a complete message is to deliver information to people about their actions, communication or behavior and your response to it in a holistic way to avoid misunderstandings and hurt. To say things in a way that people will be able hear comfortably and understand what you are saying without becoming defensive or argumentative.

Complete feedback is best kept simple, informative, honest, direct and spoken in a calm and respectful manner.

STEW

An easy way to remember the elements needed for a feedback message to be complete is to make a stew:

S See: what you notice/observe.

T Think: what you think about the situation.

E Emotion: how you feel about it.

W Want: what it is you wish/want/need or would like to happen next or in future similar situations.

> With practice, you can learn to quickly put together a complete feedback message for every occasion with family, friends, in meetings, and in most situations in the workplace.

It may take a little time to retrain yourself to not react to things that upset you. However, if you can do this, and make the effort to create and deliver your feedback to volunteers and other people in a way that they can hear it and learn from it, your relationships could improve, and you are more likely to achieve the results you want.

Delivering Complete Feedback

Make your feedback direct

You know what you really want to say, so say it directly. It's pointless assuming that people know what you think or want. People are poor mind readers; they have no idea what is going on inside you. Save yourself and everybody else, time and trouble by being direct with your feedback.

Make your feedback immediate

If you're concerned, hurt, angry or needing to change something, delaying your communication will often increase these feelings. Over time, smoldering irritation can develop into strong resentment, which can then be triggered to explode into rage. Immediate communication can quickly solve difficulties and create or improve trust. Here-and-now communications are more effective and exciting and are likely to strengthen your relationships.

Make your feedback clear

Clear feedback is a complete and accurate reflection of your observations, thoughts, feelings and needs. Avoid leaving things out, avoid being vague, and avoid being abstract or using jargon. Do not ask questions when you need to make a statement. Keep your feedback congruent, which means the content of the feedback, your tone of voice, your facial expression and your body language, all fit together and say the same thing.

Make your feedback straight

A straight piece of feedback is one in which the stated purpose is identical with the real purpose of the communication. Ask yourself a number of questions:

Q

What is it I need to say to this person, why do I need to say it and what do I want him or her to hear. Being straight means being honest, bringing the real agenda into the open, and asking for what you want or need to happen.

Use 'I' statements

Saying how you feel about something is less likely to create defensiveness in the listener than making an accusation. Saying, 'I feel upset that... ' 'I am anxious about...' 'I get concerned when...' 'I wonder what...' is easier to hear than 'you didn't...' 'You always...' 'You make me...' etc. Wherever possible avoid the word 'Why?' as this can make feedback sound like an accusation or an interrogation.

Make your feedback supportive

Q

Ask yourself, 'Do I want my feedback to be heard defensively or comfortably?' The following guidelines could be adhered to in avoiding the risk of people feeling defensive:

> ➢ Avoid using labels such as, stupid, selfish, mean, disgusting, worthless, lazy, etc.
> ➢ Avoid making accusation such as, 'You're wrong, you do everything badly, you are a difficult person.'
> ➢ Avoid using sarcasm as it demonstrates contempt.
> ➢ Avoid dragging up past similar situations. To do so might prevent any chance of clarifying how each of you feels about the present

situation.

➢ Avoid negative comparisons between people, 'you are not as efficient as…

➢ Avoid making judgmental 'you' feedback statements, 'you are… you don't… you never… you always'.

➢ Avoid making threats. Making a threat, whether or not you are able or willing to carry it out is very likely to bring co-operative communication to a screeching halt.

Make your feedback compassionate

It is unlikely that you will know the full extent of what's going on in anyone else's life. Even people you know well might have issues, concerns, thoughts and feelings that they have not disclosed to you. This is even more likely with people you don't know very well or with whom you have only a slight working relationship. There may be reasons about which you know nothing that might be affecting a person's actions and behavior.

Feedback that is given with a sense of compassion is likely to be more effective than feedback that is delivered without any thought to the recipient's situation. At the same time you could have some compassion for yourself. It may take some careful thought, self-control and sometimes courage to offer appropriate feedback and bring about the necessary changes or improvement in another person's behavior and actions.

> Offering feedback in these ways can help to avoid win/lose, good/bad, wrong /right situations.

One flowing feedback statement

It is important to deliver your complete feedback in one flowing statement without breaks or hesitation. That way all the elements of the feedback are expressed before the other person has the opportunity to make a response to just one element. This will allow that person to hear all the aspects of what you are saying, which will help him or her to receive the information without feeling the need to be defensive or to react negatively. It could also help to avoid that person experiencing feelings of hurt or disempowerment.

For the volunteer in our example scenario to understand her error in photocopying and to learn from it, constructive feedback could have been given to her in the following complete feedback message:

'I appreciate you photocopying this report so quickly. We will be able get these in the mail tonight. I notice that the paper has been photocopied on one side only. As I feel anxious that we save money wherever we can and think we ought to play our part in protecting the environment I would prefer you to do double-sided photocopying whenever possible. It's surprising what a difference can be made over a year by doing that. Let's find someone who can show you how to produce double sided copies on our machine.'

In this feedback, the volunteer is appreciated for the work she has done, is told how it could have been handled more appropriately and the reasons why and is offered some support and training to improve her skills, both for her benefit and for that of the organization.

Remember: The basic guideline for being a constructive communicator is to communicate in the way you would like to be communicated with.

Constructive Communication is described in great detail in SMART TALKING an in SMART LISTENING in the YOU MAKE THE DIFFERENCE series that are available in paperback end e-book formats from Amazon and accessible through our website: www.youmakethedifference.net

Make a note

Make a note of anywhere that the poor quality of communications are creating problems within your project, group or organization.

-

-

-

-

-

-

-

-

-

Make a note

Make a note of the ways in which all communications could be improved within your project, group or organization.

-

-

-

-

-

-

-

-

-

-

-

-

-

-

-

-

5

LEADERSHIP

Management structures

It is surprising to discover how many voluntary and community groups and organizations still manage themselves through very hieratical structures. This is perhaps understandable in places where society is still organized with traditional bureaucracy and in strict top-down management styles. It does not make so much sense in places where the structures of management, within business or governance, are flattening out and where many decisions are now made in consultation with workers or the public.

The people in leadership roles in voluntary groups and organizations are being increasingly held accountable for their actions and especially for how any money that has been donated from either public or private sources is being handled. Although this is an improvement upon some previous systems and structures that encouraged inefficiency and lax accounting and provided opportunities for poor service and even fraudulent behavior, it can result in these organizations still being run along narrow strictly hierarchical lines. This often leads to the tight control of an organization by a few; at the potential disadvantage of the many. It can also result in organizations losing many opportunities for benefitting from the leadership skills and experience they have available to them, especially from their talented volunteers.

Cooperative structures

There are now a variety of structures and systems under which voluntary groups and organizations can set themselves up, if they are being formed, or put into place if they are well established. Many structures have been created over recent years that support more cooperative working and collaborative decision-making in voluntary and community organizations.

Information on a number of these legal and managerial structures can be found in the book, SUCCESSFUL GROUPS AND PROJECTS in the YOU MAKE THE DIFFERENCE series that is available in paperback and e-book formats from Amazon and accessible through our website: www.youmakethedifference.net.

Voluntary organizations and community groups provide many opportunities for people to explore leadership. Having an understanding of what leadership means and how best to manage leadership roles within a group and organizations can be empowering for individuals and beneficial for groups organizations. This understanding might make the difference to the effectiveness of a project and even whether or not it remains sustainable.

Leadership myths

There are some myths surrounding leadership.

Myth 1 - 'Leader' is another word for 'Boss'.

The word leader can bring up a lot of emotions in people. To some people this word represents power or authority, which can be what some people want, some people shy away from having and some people resent in those who have them.

Many unfortunate attitudes have developed as a result of how the power of leadership has been used and abused in the past. One of these is the belief that anyone who is egotistical enough to want to be a leader is obviously too egotistical to be fully trusted.

It seems to me that these attitudes to leadership have no place in voluntary and community groups and organizations and it would be wise for the people in them to dispel the myth that leader means boss in their organization.

Myth 2 - 'Too many Chiefs and not enough Indians.'

This is an old saying in my culture, which, along with another, 'Too many cooks spoil the broth', warn against having too many people being involved in making decisions. This might apply in groups where there is an absence of agreed decision-making procedures or where the roles within the group are not clearly defined.

However, this myth supports the old Paradigm of leaders and followers. In this Paradigm, a leader, or a very small group of people, make the decisions and give instructions, which everyone else involved obeys or carries out. This might have merit in some situations, in organizations that deal with crisis situations for example, although this approach is unlikely to prove to be the best method for empowering people in voluntary organizations and community groups.

The new Paradigm of mutual support and cooperation encourages people to see themselves as leaders in appropriate situations and empowers them to confidently step up to take some responsibility when necessary. This is more likely to achieve better results in voluntary organizations and community groups.

Leadership Styles

There are a variety of leadership styles each having benefits and disadvantages and each being appropriate for particular circumstances. Some are more effective than others and it is often apparent that a person's leadership style is an extension of their personality. These styles mostly fall into one of the following categories: authoritarian, democratic, facilitating.

A. Authoritarian

Authoritarian leaders lead from the top down and might be dictatorial towards their group members. They can be rigid in their thinking and may be difficult to deal with when disagreed with.

The other attributes that often come along with authoritarian leadership might hold a project back from fulfilling its full potential. These characteristics can include: pride, self-importance, self-righteousness and a sense of superiority. These can result in a number of situations:

1. The leader's unwillingness or inability to listen to the advice, suggestions and ideas of others.
2. Their unwillingness to delegate functions and decision-making to others.
3. Their lack of patience and tolerance that undermines or disempowers group members, workers and volunteers.
4. Their inability to recognize their own poor communication skills.
5. Their inability to inspire good communications within the project or group.
6. Their unrealistically high assessment of their own skills and abilities.
7. Their inaccurately low opinion of the skills and abilities of the other people involved.

Authoritarianism is sometimes confused with strong leadership. From my experience it is rarely strong leadership. In fact, any need a leader might have to be dictatorial, to get their own way or to bully people into submission is usually based upon their own insecurities and the fear that these will be exposed. There is nothing strong in that!

However, an authoritarian style of leadership - preferably without the negative attributes - might be vital in some critical or dangerous situations where people need to be clearly guided or instructed in what to do.

B. Democratic Leadership

Democratic leaders are likely to delegate some of the leadership responsibilities to others in the group. They will work with those involved to set up systems and structures to empower people. They will solicit ideas, suggestions and proposals, encourage discussion, and include as many as is feasible in decision-making. Within the group, the majority rules most of the time, although, this type of leader might occasionally exercise their veto during voting.

> Democratic leadership is most applicable for encouraging cooperation and creating a culture that will support people to take the initiative and for positive group development.

C. Facilitating Leadership

Some leaders seem hardly to be leaders at all. They appear to have very little formal influence upon most aspects of the group's activities, which they trust to be handled by the people who have taken responsibility for them. When they facilitate discussion and decision-making they are likely to choose to forego any power of veto. They maintain an overall view and understanding of what is happening in the project and ensure that information throughout the organization is disseminated in an appropriate and timely manner.

Facilitating leadership is most suitable when a group has reached the cooperative stage in its development and those in the group have confidence and trust in themselves and in each other. Involvement from these leaders will then mostly be in mentoring, supporting and encouraging members of the group as they carry out their tasks.

Each of these styles will be suitable for specific circumstances.

Leading volunteers

Whether you are a volunteer who is coordinating a small group of other local volunteers or a manager of hundreds or even thousands of volunteers in a national or international organization – you are a leader. How you carry out that leadership role will have a significant impact upon those volunteers, upon their enjoyment and effectiveness of their volunteer activities and upon the success of the project or organization.

It is vital to always remember that volunteers are offering their time, skills and expertise for the benefit of others and in support of the aims of the project. These people are likely to thrive on encouragement and mutual respect.

When people feel recognized for their abilities and trusted to use those abilities effectively they are more likely to continue to do so than when feeling doubted, distrusted overly managed or controlled.

Volunteers are likely to be less effective when attitudes of criticism and disrespect lead to their feelings of disempowerment. This also applies to negative attitudes, which can be harmful to the survival of any group. Negative attitudes could include: defeatism, aggression, undermining, sabotaging and the seeking of scapegoats.

> Attitudes that would be helpful in a group situation are: Cooperation, open-mindedness, honest and direct communication and compassion.

Loyalty and leadership

Wise people in leadership roles know to place loyalty high on the agenda for achievement, and they set the example for loyalty within their organization. They demonstrate loyalty at every opportunity: to the project, to the group or organization's principles and agreements and most especially to every group member. Through this example, loyalty can become automatic among staff and volunteers and an intrinsic part of the organization's culture.

It seems to me that within voluntary and community groups and organizations, there is no place for the 'us' and 'them' attitudes of separation that exist in many hierarchical structures. This sense of separation more easily allows for blame to be placed rather than cooperative remedies to be sought. Voluntary and Community Groups, Organizations and Associations thrive on the belief that, 'we are all in this together'. Everyone in a group can contribute towards this sense of togetherness.

> For a group, team or activity leader in a voluntary or community group to be most effective, he or she, would be wise to use more elements of mentoring than managing, and place a greater emphasis on facilitation and coaching than upon controlling.

Timing

An important part of being an effective leader is the comprehension of right timing.

Understanding the timing of strategies. Knowing when it is the right time to initiate a discussion or a process. Understanding the appropriate times to intervene or to hold back.

There are likely to be times when changes need to be made to the structure to fulfill the objectives of the project or even to guarantee its survival. Any lack of ability on the part of anyone in any leadership role to recognize when the project has grown to the point where major changes are necessary could seriously restrict the projects potential.

Being open to feedback in leadership roles

It may take a lot of courage for volunteers to bring their concerns and distress about the quality of leadership to the notice of someone in a leadership role, especially an authoritarian leader, and yet, it might be difficult for the group or organization to be effective or even to survive if this is not done.

There are a number of ways in which concerns of this nature can be brought out into the open. The choice of which will depend upon the make-up of the group, how communications within an organization are conducted and the personality of the leader:

Options:
  a. Procedures could be put in place for dealing with concerns and complaints.
  b. Complaints and concerns can be brought up in regular group meetings.
  c. Special meetings could be called in which they can be presented.

The seven C's of leadership

For leadership to be most effective it would be useful to consider the seven C's of leadership:

1. Commitment.
2. Creativity.
3. Communication.
4. Collaboration.
5. Co-operation.
6. Consensus.
7. Courage.

Commitment

Leadership and commitment go hand-in-hand. Leadership commitment means not only saying that you are committed to a principle, to a cause, to aims and outcomes or to a group of people; it requires a demonstration of that commitment. If you are not committed to the organization, to the goals of the group, to the outcome of a project or to those people with whom you are working, then how can you expect others to be?

> Showing commitment to any of these is a demonstration of leadership.

Creativity

Leadership often requires creative thinking. Whether that is thinking laterally, thinking outside the box, recognizing options and opportunities or encouraging creative thinking in others.

> These aspects of creative thinking are demonstrations of leadership.

Communication

Effective leadership depends upon effective communication. Whether that is delivering instructions; succinctly getting ideas across; clearly stating the reality of a situation or encouraging and supporting the constructive communication of other people.

> Being a good communicator in any of these areas is a demonstration of leadership.

Collaboration

This form of leadership means working collaboratively with people in the team; bringing people together in groups to work in mutual support of one another or seeking collaboration from people outside the group or organization.

> A person able to inspire collaboration with and from others is demonstrating leadership.

Cooperation

Empowering leadership inspires cooperative working. The leader who does not work cooperatively with people in their team is likely to be more of a dictator than a leader. A leader who does not seek cooperation from those outside of the group may lead the group into a place of isolation and alienation from those whose support would be helpful or necessary.

> A person who is able to encourage and maintain co-operation within a group and/or is able to attract cooperation from others outside of the group is demonstrating leadership.

Consensus

Leadership does not mean making all the decisions. Inspiring, supportive and empowering leadership results from ensuring that those who will carry out decisions have had a hand in making them, preferably, through consensus.

> A person encouraging and/or facilitating consensus decision making in a group is demonstrating leadership.

Courage

It often takes courage for a person to step into a leadership role. It can require courage to take a stand on an issue or to say the things that need to be said when mindful of the potential consequences. It may need courage to take on responsibility. Especially if other people do not recognize there is some responsibility to take; if the person might not be perceived as the obvious person to take it; or when others are unable or unwilling to do so.

> The willingness to step forward in any of these circumstances is a demonstration of leadership.

You can make the difference

You could be an example of leadership that would offer encouragement to others to find or develop their leadership qualities. It can often just take one person to make a significant difference to a group by doing something different, to take the initiative, to speak up, to ask a question, to make a suggestion, to be positive and supportive.

Encouraging leadership among volunteers

Encouraging volunteers to step into leadership roles is beneficial to them and to the organization. Having people available who feel empowered to take the initiative whenever appropriate or necessary can safeguard the sustainability of a project.

It is useful to remember that having people who are confident in their abilities to handle responsibility and who feel trusted and supported by their colleagues from all levels of the organization can spread the load of leadership for the benefit of everyone concerned.

Leadership is not only required in areas of management and function. There are other aspects of leadership that impact the effectiveness and sustainability of any group. These aspects are about influencing the attitudes and behavior of fellow members and the culture of the group. This form of leadership is more about demonstrating cooperative and supportive ways of being and modeling the attitudes, behavior and methods of personal communication that inspire others and encourage group cohesion. It includes a willingness to take responsibility, not only for a function or an activity, also for one's thoughts, words and deeds and the consequences of any of these.

Being championed by colleagues to step into leadership roles can be enormously encouraging for volunteers considering taking on some aspect of leadership. Especially when this occurs in a group culture devoid of blame where successes are acknowledged and failures are seen as learning opportunities. Volunteers will be even more encouraged when being championed and supported to do so by someone in a managerial position, a person they consider to be a leader.

Everyone is a potential leader

This is not just warm and fuzzy language! It is my belief based upon decades of experience.

> It seems obvious that in any situation the person with the appropriate skills, the appropriate information and/or experience; who has the appropriate attitude and intention and is willing to step forward at the appropriate time, is the obvious leader in that situation.

Whether or not the obvious person takes up any leadership role in a situation is usually dependent upon their **courage, confidence and willingness** to pick up that leadership baton at that time, and, whether the people they would be leading are willing to allow them to do so.

Being courageous

It may take courage for a person to offer himself or herself as a leader in a situation. Especially if they are new to a group or if there is significant or obvious difference between them and the other members, such as age, gender, ethnic background, religion etc. A potential leader might be concerned that any action they would recommend might be unpopular with the rest of the group. If a person has seen others who have put themselves forward for leadership being metaphorically shot at, it may take great courage for them to risk putting themselves in the same position.

Being confident

For most of us, confidence in our abilities and in ourselves in general can take a long time to develop and yet can so quickly be undermined. I have seen talented people join groups with the very best of intentions, only to find their confidence in their abilities being eroded by the judgmental culture of the group and the critical and unsupportive attitudes of the members.

In some organizations it may take a lot of self-confidence for some people to offer their skills, knowledge or experience in some leadership capacity, especially in those organizations which have a blame culture, where there is little mutual trust and loyalty or where the word 'leader' is assumed to mean boss.

Being willing

The willingness to take on the responsibility for leadership is what makes someone **into** a leader even if it's only for a short while or in particular circumstances.

Developing leadership strengths

Developing leadership qualities in your volunteers will be of great benefit to them; it can make your job easier and more rewarding and is likely to create all sorts of opportunities for win-win situations for the volunteers and for the organization.

It is worth remembering that many of your volunteer's activities can offer opportunities for them to practice communicating clearly and to try out ways of getting their ideas across, and for respectfully challenging statements or situations about which they have concerns. You could support them to practice and to gain courage and confidence in these areas.

In any area of development, the trick is to keep on keeping on. This is why the support of others is so valuable. It can prevent people from feeling alone and vulnerable and from doubting themselves, giving up or slipping into a decline if things don't go so well. You could encourage your volunteers to seek support in the development of their leadership skills from a mentor or you might help them to find other people who would be willing to engage with them in mutual peer support. These could be people in the same group or those who have no involvement in it. You might help volunteers to find others who are struggling with some of the same issues or they could perhaps find people who, although dealing with entirely different issues, would value some mutual support.

It is important to remember that any moves forward in developing your volunteer's leadership skills need only be made in tiny steps. No giant leaps are needed or recommended.

Help your volunteers to take a small step in one of the areas in which they wish to improve and see how it feels. If something works well, encourage them to do more of it. If something doesn't work well, support them to do something different next time. If something your volunteer's engage in feels too uncomfortable for them, explore with them why that might be. It could be just that the step they have taken was a bit too big at this point.

With practice, the levels of your volunteer's courage, confidence and willingness will grow. They will probably begin to wonder why they ever had any doubts about themselves or their leadership abilities. After some time, you might observe your volunteers effortlessly assuming leadership roles that have potential for making a positive difference to the organization's effectiveness.

> It only takes one person to show the way for an organization to consist of people who are willing to take responsibility for making things happen, who are able to step into appropriate leadership roles whenever necessary while having the support and confidence of the other members, and to encourage others to do the same.

This is the real power of leadership.

Make a list

Make a list of the areas and occasions where you could encourage leadership potential in your volunteers.

-

-

-

-

-

-

-

-

-

-

-

-

-

6

PROVIDING ONGOING SUPPORT

It is beneficial, and in many situations essential, to have mechanisms in place for you to understand how effective your volunteers are being and how fulfilled they feel.

Options:
1. Put feedback systems in place for volunteers to keep you informed of their progress, of their thoughts and feelings about their work and the project and what support they need to be fully effective.
2. Provide easy means for your volunteers to request support and to offer suggestions for improvements and ideas for project development.
3. One volunteer could be given the role of liaising with their colleagues and sharing the information they are given throughout the group. In a larger organization, such a person could sit in management meetings to feedback progress, concerns and suggestions from the volunteers. They would report back to their volunteer colleagues on the meetings that they had attended.
4. A volunteer with experience of management could become a coordinator of volunteers in some organizations. It is important for any volunteer manager, coordinator or liaison person to be part of the management group. This raises the image of volunteering.

An inclusive way of offering support is through regular meetings or gatherings with your volunteers. These can provide volunteers with opportunities to share with one another and with managers the highs and lows and the success and concerns of their volunteering experience. They can learn from one another's experiences; provide support to one another; and offer to each other, and to the managers, suggestions for dealing with problems and difficult situations. Such meetings could also keep volunteers updated with news and important information.

Make a note

Make a note of any new mechanisms that could be put in place for you to understand how effective your volunteers are being and how fulfilled they feel.

-

-

-

-

-

-

-

-

-

-

-

-

-

Mutual Support Groups

These offer simple and effective methods to assist people to be supportive to one another. Mutual Support is offered within a group setting of a handful of people. If a voluntary group has only a few members then they could probably all participate in the process in one group. If the project or organizations has more than a handful of volunteers then these could be divided into small groups of between 4 and 6 people per group.

In a Mutual Support Group meeting people are given the space to think out loud on various aspects of their work.

Remember: All the benefits of having equal opportunities to speak in an interruption free setting are obviously vital during Mutual Support Group meetings.

Description

Each person in the group in turn considers out loud the following four questions:

Q

Question one: What is going well for me as a volunteer in this project/group/organization? (Whichever is appropriate)

Question two: What is difficult for me as a volunteer with this project/group/organization?

Question three: How does this affect my intentions as a volunteer with this project/group/organization?

Question four: As a volunteer with this project/group/organization what are my next achievable steps in dealing with these difficulties and moving towards fulfilling these intentions?

Why these questions?

Each of the questions is included for a number of reasons:

Q

1. What is going well for me?

This causes the person speaking to think of the positive aspects of their voluntary work and reminds them of their capacity to do well. This is a valuable first step, which opens proceedings in the opposite way to the more usual form of leaping straight forward into grumbles about the difficulties in situations. The habit of complaining first is deeply ingrained in many people and the Mutual Support method always seeks to stand this tendency on its head.

Q

2. What is difficult for me?

This question now takes place in the context of the thoughts expressed in the 'what's going well?' question. This reduces the power that difficulties have to hold a person back from being fulfilled or effective in their volunteering. However, having the opportunity to talk about difficulties, especially within a group of people with common aims, is always welcome as both speaker and listeners can gain fresh perspectives as a result.

Q

3. How do these experiences fit with my intentions?

This question gives the opportunity for reflection rather than complaint. It offers people an opportunity to verbalize whether or not their current experience is matching their intentions for volunteering and the needs they wish it to fulfill. They are not expected to know how they will bring about any solutions beyond identifying the next step.

Q

4. What are my next available steps?

When the person speaking works with this, he or she is identifying practical steps to take towards solving the specific problem they are dealing with or for achieving their overall volunteering goals and needs. If these steps are taken then real progress for change and improvement is likely to be made.

> Note: The emphasis is on 'my next achievable steps' and not on identifying any steps that others could or 'should' take. However, the next steps might entail requesting or suggesting alterations in current systems or procedures.

Explanations

When running through the four questions the facilitator of this process gives people the rationale as described above for including each one. A copy of the four questions can be given to each group or to each participant or written up somewhere visible.

It is a great help if people are already familiar with Constructive

Communication processes. This way they will know the requirements for and the benefits of speaking clearly and openly and giving good attention to each other. If not, facilitators could explain these.

Support Group process

➢ Groups of three to six people are created.

➢ A timekeeper is appointed from among them.

➢ The first person thinks and speaks out loud about each of the questions in order, whilst the others listen attentively. The object of the exercise is for the person speaking to hear him or herself think about their situation and come up with steps to make any necessary improvement in their volunteering experience.

➢ Nobody interrupts, no questions are asked – unless for clarity of understanding - and no explanations or justifications are required. Everyone in the group just gives good attention to the speaker. (If support in identifying next steps is requested by the speaker the other members of the group can offer suggestions and other forms of help).

➢ Then it is the turn of the next person to work through the questions.

➢ Strict timekeeping is used and people may need to be prompted by the timekeeper.

➢ It is important that all members remain in support of one another and that the content of what is said is kept confidential unless an agreement is made otherwise.

Timing

Allowing a specific amount of time for each question concentrates the mind wonderfully. It helps people to think and to speak concisely and helps to avoid waffling, hesitation and procrastination. The timing of the questions will depend on how many are in the group and how much time is available for the event.

For a group of four people, each taking two minutes for each question, this process will take around thirty-five minutes, allowing for a short, respectful handover period between speakers. If this meeting is a regular check in then this amount of time might be sufficient, which means that, with some additional time for greetings and partings, a meeting could be successfully concluded well within an hour.

Often however, a group may have more than four members and some people might need extra time to talk through one or more questions and there could be a need for some supportive option identification of next steps. It might be advisable to allow a longer amount of time in order for the process to be fully supportive.

Identifying options

If a person is experiencing difficulties in identifying some next achievable steps then he or she might be open to suggestions of options from the group. This is not an excuse for other members of the group to launch forth with directions on what to do. Care needs to be taken to respectfully suggest options in a manner that leaves the person in control of their process. Suggested options could be offered in a Go–Round or in a short Brainstorming session.

It is always wise to avoid such statements as 'Why don't you...' or 'If I were you...'

Seeking practical help

Sometimes people need some practical help to achieve their next steps. This help might be offered from within the group. Or through a group discussion or Brainstorming session other options for obtaining that help might be identified.

Benefits

Many people have little opportunity to think in such a supportive, reflective way. This method gives them an opportunity to consider the reality of their situation and to practice thinking strategically. The fact that the process can be conducted in quite a short space of time is one of its benefits.

It is useful to remember that more of the considerable benefits of this process might only be fully appreciated through the experience of it.

Challenges

a. Some people may have difficulties in openly reflecting upon their volunteer goals or acknowledging the needs they wish to fulfill through their voluntary activities. This might be due to their belief that they have no business in having volunteering goals or no right to have needs that could be fulfilled through volunteering. When people are working with the Mutual Support process they may find it useful to notice that they are really claiming their right to feel fulfilled in their voluntary work and that their own goals and intentions for this work are valid.

b. For organizations to allocate time for their volunteers to participate in a Mutual Support group within the volunteer's working time, especially in a busy and perhaps over-stretched voluntary organization might be a challenge to achieve.

c. Suggesting that volunteers allocate some of their time for being part of a Mutual Support Group outside of their volunteering activities might also be received with less than enthusiastic agreement.

d. In both these cases people may need some convincing that spending time on this is valuable. After a while however, groups may find this process so beneficial that they will wish to participate regularly in this form of mutual support, for example once a month or so.

When Mutual Support Group meetings become established as part of an organization's culture this can have significant results and benefits.

Within larger meetings

A Mutual Support process could be a component part of a longer meeting or event where information is to be shared with volunteers or future strategies are to be considered.

A similar process could be used in a number of ways:
1. A process within a meeting to ensure that each participant achieves at least part of his or her desired outcome for that meeting.
2. As a group method to identify reasons for a project being stuck and generating ideas for moving it forward.
3. As a way for groups to support one another's potential and to encourage action.

Small Mutual Support Groups can be formed within larger meetings so that people with similar goals or needs can support one another.

Independent Mutual Support Groups

People who volunteer with different projects or groups from one another could also form Mutual Support Groups. These people need have no common interests beyond volunteering and no common goals other than wanting to be mutually supportive to one another.

Practice makes perfect

The capacity to work in this way increases significantly with practice. The practical benefits which appear when people act upon their next achievable steps are clear evidence that speaking intentions out loud in a supportive environment is an effective method for turning concerns into actions for improvement.

Receiving ideas and suggestions

For most projects to stay alive and growing, ideas and suggestions need to be encouraged from all those involved.

> Beware of believing that all your advisers need to be professionals from outside of your organization. Your most valuable advisers might very well be those working within the organization. That includes the volunteers.

These are likely to be the people 'on the ground' and to be the ones interfacing with the people who your organization is committed to helping. To ignore suggestions and ideas from volunteers might be a waste of opportunities and resources.

Options:
1. Have simple processes for collecting and considering ideas and suggestions from volunteers.
2. Have easy methods, such as creating Mutual Support Groups, to help with the exploration of these ideas and suggestions and for creating the steps to implement them.

Ideas people
Sometimes the people who have useful ideas and suggestions are not necessarily the ones best equipped to carry them out. The kind of thinking it takes to see the bigger picture may not be the kind to work out the details. On the other hand an observer of some particular problem might not see how this fits into the overall plan.

> It often takes one set of skills to initiate a project, another set to maintain it and yet another set to effectively support and manage the people involved.

For a number of years I worked with someone who chaired a community project. His response to ideas and suggestions from group members was 'how are you going to make that happen?'

While I realize that this was his way of encouraging people to take responsibility for making their ideas work, I noticed that it often had the opposite effect. After a while, the people with the brightest and most useful ideas and suggestions stopped offering them out of concern that they would be obliged to develop their suggestions and to commit time, effort and perhaps skills they did not have.

Many of those who tried to turn their ideas into reality failed to do so or were only partially effective. This often left them feeling inadequate and usually resulted in them keeping future ideas and suggestions to themselves.

If having ideas and making suggestions is what some people are good at, they could be appreciated for those skills alone. They perhaps might act as advisors on the implementing of their ideas while other people with the appropriate skill sets put the suggestions into action.

Make a note

Make a note of new systems that could be implemented to gather ideas and suggestion from your volunteers.

-

-

-

-

-

-

-

-

-

-

-

-

-

-

-

-

-

-

-

-

Effective meetings

As identified in the previous section, one of the simplest ways of receiving ideas from volunteers is through regular meetings.

Of course there are many reasons for calling meetings. There may be new information to be shared. There might be choices to identify and make decisions about, methods, systems, processes and procedures to be reviewed, strategies for ongoing work or development to be discussed. Regular meetings may be required as set down in an organization's Articles of Association.

Meetings can be contentious issues amongst volunteers, (and other people for that matter!). Some people might think that there are not enough meetings held in their group or organization. These people may feel that they are not included in decisions being made that affect them or that their views are not valued or respected by those at a management level.

Others might think meetings are a waste of time that get in the way of the 'real' work or that it's unfair to ask volunteers to commit time to meetings during their volunteered time and unreasonable to expect them to do so in their own time.

Opinions differ about meetings, not only for these reasons. Often people's opinion about the usefulness or validity of meetings is based upon their past experiences of them. Some meetings are productive and enjoyable while others can be frustrating or inconclusive. An individual's experience of past meetings is likely to influence how they approach future meetings.

As more people become engaged in community activities and volunteer their time with organizations that are endeavoring to make a difference, they are likely to be required to attend meetings. It would be helpful to them for these meetings to be effective, productive and enjoyable.

> Well-managed meetings can save any organization huge amounts of time, effort and resources. Understanding the effective ways of participating in meetings will help those participating in them to make the most of their time and can prevent frustration and wasted effort and resources.

This is why the first book that I wrote in the YOU MAKE THE DIFFERENCE series was ENJOYABLE & EFFECTIVE MEETINGS, which offers guidelines, information and insights for effective participation, various methods of meeting management and ways of handling tricky situations. The second book in this series, EFFORTLESS FACILITATION focuses on all aspects of facilitation: planning meetings and events; useful procedures, methods and processes; and some ready-made meeting designs to fit many situations. These books are available in paperback and e-book formats from Amazon and are accessible through our website: www.youmakethedifference.net

You could make a huge difference to the effectiveness of your project, group or organization by championing an effective and enjoyable meeting culture.

7

MANAGING VOLUNTEERS

It will be clear by now that I think the most appropriate method of managing volunteers is through supporting and empowering them to be as effective as possible. In organizations that have large numbers of volunteers some professional management is likely to be needed. In bigger organizations, having someone in the role of Volunteer Manager is helpful, often vital, for the attracting, recruiting, supporting and retaining of volunteers.

The recognition of the importance of this role is growing and training in the systems and methods for improving the skill levels of the people in volunteer management are becoming more available in institutions, colleges and universities.

Sometimes people with Human Resources backgrounds are appointed to the role of managing volunteers. There is some logic to this, although, so is some need for caution. Some Human Resources principles and processes do not transfer well to the Voluntary and Community Sector. Many of the ways of supporting volunteers to be effective are quite different from those methods used in managing employees.

Obviously, the main differences between paid employees and volunteers are that volunteers have no entitlements: no pay, no holidays, no financial incentive and no pension plan.

Remember: volunteers are giving freely of their time and experience, which is to be greatly appreciated. Using the supportive methods described in the previous chapter could help managers to encourage and support their volunteers.

Include your volunteers

Find ways of including volunteers in the progress of the organization. Keep them up-to-date with what's happening. Have regular meetings for them to be updated and for them to keep you aware of their progress, concerns, successes and suggestions. Have staff meetings that include the volunteer's representatives.

Volunteering does not mean amateur.

There has been a tendency in the past for some people to consider volunteers to be amateur or unprofessional. Unfortunately, in some cases this criticism is valid. However, in my experience, most volunteers are skilled, experienced and very professional in their approach and working practices.

Many volunteers come from backgrounds where a high level of professionalism was essential to their success. Such people will want to bring this level of professionalism to their volunteer roles. It is important that the organization is set up to allow for and to encourage this. Encouraging individuals to strive for excellence in their volunteer work and actively supporting them to do so will be of benefit to them and to the organization.

Treating volunteers, especially those highly skilled and experienced, as valuable members of the team, equal to equivalently skilled paid staff can raise the status of those volunteers and improve others perception of them.

It could be vital to your continued success for funders and statutory bodies to recognize the professionalism of your volunteers.

Volunteering and paid employment

There may be some uneasiness or even embarrassment in an organization regarding how much work volunteers do and how hard they work. This might lead to a tendency towards paying volunteers in order to keep them or to reward them for their dedication and commitment. They are then no longer volunteers! It is important to establish the difference between paid employment and volunteering. This is the difference between cats and dogs: both are loved and yet they are never to be confused with one another.

However, there is something to be said for an experienced volunteer within the organization who is familiar with the procedures and who has the necessary skills being appointed to a paid post that becomes vacant and so becoming an employee.

Replacing paid employees with volunteers.

In larger organizations, most of the essential roles are likely to be held by paid employees. In small projects and groups, most, possible all, of the roles will be handled by volunteers, although, sometimes funding might be forthcoming to pay a person playing a key role. As the financial squeeze is felt more keenly in the forthcoming years, the funding for paid staff might become reduced and be even more difficult to secure. When funding is tight or has been cut there may be temptation or even necessity to seek a person to volunteer to a role instead of a paid employee.

Strategies:

a. If this becomes a necessity it might be sensible to have more than one volunteer in any essential role. Job sharing would be an ideal strategy to ensure that more than one person has a handle on what is happening and that vital work is carried out within the necessary timeframe. I have observed that within a paid workforce the benefits of job sharing can far outweigh any of its disadvantages. For an unpaid workforce, where the disadvantage of doubling up on pension provision etc., does not exist, the benefits can be substantial.

b. There is another strategy that works well within teams of paid employees, which could be vital in teams of volunteers. It is that of having overlapping circles of information and responsibility of the team members. Each person on the team has the responsibility for specific tasks and probably has the greatest amount of expertise in that field. However, at least one, preferably two other team members could have enough skill around that task and information on its progress to be able to take it over if the main task holder is not available.

While this book is intended to support the enormous advantages of working with volunteers, there are occasions when it could be wise to be aware of the potential consequences of having a volunteer take the place of a paid person. In some circumstances this might be unwise practice. It may not be ethical and could be detrimental in several ways. It might set up resentment within the paid workforce and create ill feeling towards the chosen volunteer, which may rub off onto attitudes towards other volunteers.

If the role is essential to the effectiveness of the organization then it could be inappropriate to give such a role to someone who has no employment contract. Even though many volunteers are dedicated to the purpose of their organization and may well have a strong work ethic, with the best will in the world, volunteers, who have no tangible benefits to receive from the organization, cannot be expected to always be as fully committed to regular work as someone with a contract of employment. A volunteer's heart may actually be more in the organization than a paid employee, however the reality of life is that volunteers are at liberty to make choices that employees are not. Volunteers often have other commitments and priorities that call for their attention. It may also be ultimately disadvantageous to the project.

It would be wise to remember that once funding for a particular role has been seen to be no longer needed it will be nearly impossible to get funding for that role in the future.

Supervision

I believe that anyone who offers personal care and support to people and in whom trust is placed can greatly benefit from having access to some supervision. This not only applies to employees, for whom receiving regular supervision is often part of an employment agreement, it also applies to volunteers in charities and voluntary organizations whose work and activities can often be difficult and demanding.

Offering supervision to volunteers can bring concerns, conflicts and problems to light. These can then be addressed appropriately to avoid volunteers feeling overwhelmed or needing to carry burdens of responsibilities or difficulties alone.

In this context, supervision does not refer to the overseeing of people by a person who is a step further up the hierarchical ladder. For people, especially volunteers, in the helping and supporting fields, supervision is to be as much, if not more, for their support, as it is of the quality and efficiency of their work.

Although some aspects of supervision are similar to the principle and practices of coaching, the focus in supervision is to help people be more effective and content in their work.

Functions of Supervision

Supervision has three main functions: educational, managerial and support.

Some goals of supervision:
1. To ensure quality of work.
2. To facilitate clear communication in working relationships.
3. To manifest inspiration.
4. To appropriately focus passion.
5. To illuminate the flow of spirit in daily work and life.

Here are some more detailed goals as described on Page 59 of Supervision in the Helping Professions, Hawkins and Shohet, 2006:

a. To provide a regular opportunity for the supervisee to reflect upon the content and the process of their work.
b. To develop understanding and skills.
c. To receive information and another perspective concerning their work.
d. To receive feedback on content and process.
e. To receive validation and support both as a person and as a worker.
f. To ensure that as a person and as a worker that person is not left to carry, unnecessarily or alone, any difficulties, problems and projections regarding their work.
g. To provide space to explore and express personal distress brought up by work.
h. To effectively utilize personal and professional resources.
i. To be proactive rather than reactive.
j. To support the development and achievement of personal and organizational goals.

When supervising volunteers it is important to remember that they are gifting their time, skills and experience to the organization, and for the benefit of the organization, without any of the entitlements enjoyed by paid employees. Some focus needs to be concentrated on supporting them to gain satisfaction from their work and a sense of achievement from the results of their labors.

Benefits

Supervision has many benefits both for the volunteer and for the organization. Enabling volunteers to make the most effective use of their contribution can benefit all concerned.

Challenges

Unless volunteers are clear about the benefits to them of supervision sessions they might consider these to be a waste of their valuable time. Some people might resent being required to do something beyond the work they have committed to doing. This might result in the sessions being less effective and beneficial than they could be. Some volunteers might not see the point of supervision. They may be suspicious of the motives behind it or feel uncomfortable at the thought of speaking openly about themselves. These people might choose to avoid or refuse supervision.

> It is imperative that volunteers see supervision as a practical offer of support to them. They might need encouragement to attend sessions and help to recognize supervision as being for their benefit. As with paid employees, sessions ought to be offered within agreed working time; not extra to it.

Contracting

In most kinds of relationships, exploring intentions, visions, desires and expectations, and reaching appropriate agreements, are helpful. With supervision at work, whether that is paid or voluntary, clear contracting is usually essential. It is important that some form of contracting is entered into between the supervisor and the supervisee.

Most issues that arise in supervision have both personal and organizational implications. Figuring out which is which, and understanding the relationship between the two, is at the heart of the work. Having a clearer understanding about who is talking and what intentions, expectations and needs are present, the more fruitful the supervising conversation will be.

Areas that need definition and clarification in the contracting:

Purpose

1. What is the purpose of the conversation - is this line supervision or support coaching?
2. What are we doing here now - the immediate conversation?
3. What might be the wider implications?
4. Is there an agreed purpose?
5. What does the supervisee hope to gain?
6. Does the supervisor have an agenda of items to be covered?

Time
- How long is available for the sessions?
- How will that time, the management of the agenda, the feedback, etc. be structured?

Style
- Will the session entail questions? Listening? Advising?

Needs
a. What are the needs of the supervisee?
b. What are the needs of the supervisor?
c. What are the needs of the organization?
d. What are the needs of the vocation of volunteering?

Confidentiality
1. What confidentiality agreements will be made?
2. How will these affect and be affected by needs?

Organizational context
- What is the supervisee's role, job description, etc.?
- What are their responsibilities?
- Who is paying for the session?
- Who is responsible to whom?
- Who has an interest in this session, what is that interest and what are the implications?
- Who has a claim to know what?
- How does this affect confidentiality?

Outcomes
a. How will we know when we have finished the session/the work?
b. How might we know this has been successful and beneficial?
c. What are the indicators and consequences of success and failure?

It can be useful to consider what is sometimes referred to as Good Will Contracting. This would be creating agreements about working with such things as gossip, both the positive and negative aspects of this and how people talk about and refer to themselves, especially in public.

It is important to resist any temptation or internal pressure or the pressure from the supervisee or the organization, to move past these contracting issues and to go straight into dealing with 'the business' of the session. Contracting is about boundaries and boundaries are important elements of the business of supervision. Time spent in clear contracting is invaluable. In fact, there is perhaps a sense in which contracting sums up the whole business of supervision.

Having said that; it is useful to remember that nothing is written in stone. It is always possible and frequently essential to revisit and refine these agreements as a session or working relationship evolves.

The supervision session

Supervision is usually conducted through the asking of appropriate questions. These will have different purposes and uses:

    a.   To acquire specific information, 'what is your role?'
    b.   To encourage someone to say more about something, 'how is that work carried out?'
    c.   To invite someone to open up, 'what's happening with …?'
    d.   To check things out, 'I notice you are frowning, I wonder if that means you are angry?'
    e.   Soliciting an opinion, 'what do you think about that?'
    f.   Enquiring about feelings, 'how do you feel about that?'

It is useful to distinguish between questions that are more open and questions that are more closed. Open questions are invitations to open up more communication and expand on information, 'can you say more about that?' Closed questions such as 'do you…?' often result in only 'yes' or 'no' answers that limit further conversation. Although they are often restrictive, they might occasionally be used to clarify specific points, 'do you mean…?'

There are of course many kinds of question that lie between these two ends of the scale.

Focusing questions
These help to define the conflict or problem:

Q

'What did he say that led you to this conclusion?' 'How does this relate to your experience here?' These sorts of question can also help to separate out issues, 'shall we work on this issue before going into the next thing?'

Q

Defining questions
These help move past generalizations, 'when you say "people", do you mean all people?' 'Which people are you referring to? 'You say "always", are

there times when this doesn't happen?' 'Can you really not think of a single person who…?'

Q

Questions to uncover underlying issues

These gently probe for feelings, anxieties or even dreams, etc., which are under the surface and fuelling the emotional process, 'what is important to you about this?' 'What does it feel like to be in that situation?' 'What's the sense you have about this?'

Q

Challenging questions

These are invitations for self-reflection and for the supervisee to share more information, thoughts and feelings about a particular situation or area of work: 'that sounds important, say more about that.' 'What usually happens then?' 'Could there be 1% of truth in the feedback you received?' 'Can you imagine anything in your behavior that warrants her kind of response?'

Questions can be thought of as tools that can shape responses and the direction in which the conversation moves. Because of this, care needs to be taken to avoid mistakenly leading a supervisee along a path of discussion that you believe is appropriate rather than the one that would be most valuable.

The importance of listening

In my experience the quality of a supervisor's work will be affected by the quality of his or her listening. Constructive Listening in supervision will be greatly beneficial to the supervisee and the supervisor.

Who can supervise?

Supervision is often an internal function of an organization and might even be specific to a particular work area. It can be helpful to have a supervisor from within the department/organization who would therefore be aware of the functions and the challenges facing the supervisees. On the other hand, people from outside the work area or the organization sometimes carry out supervision. This has the advantage of the supervisor possibly maintaining a more independent and neutral attitude and bringing a wider perspective to the role.

Supervision as a voluntary contribution

The skills and experience of supervision could be offered as a voluntary contribution to charities, voluntary organizations and community groups by individuals who wish to be supportive of the aims of those groups or organizations. This may be a way for organizations to offer supervision to their volunteers and for volunteers to receive beneficial support that otherwise might not be available to them.

Experienced supervisors could also offer valuable voluntary supervisory support to paid employees in charities and community projects who, perhaps through lack of funding, would not otherwise have access to this sort of support. This could be of great benefit to those in leadership positions who might feel isolated in their role and have no one with whom to share the burden of their responsibilities.

An example of volunteered supervision

This is my experience of when I received valuable voluntary supervision from Joan Wilmot from the Centre for Supervision and Team Development, during the four years that I held the elected post of Listener Convener to the Findhorn Community.

Background

Since the early 1960s the Findhorn Community has been an interesting and inspiring place for personal, spiritual and community development. In the later years this interest and inspiration has expanded to include Ecovillage development and social, economic and environmental sustainability.

These were years of great changes within the Community as new structures and decision-making processes were created and the broadening of Community membership took place.

The role of Listener Convener

The role of Listener Convener is to have a finger on the pulse of the Community and to be the ears of the Community. To be the person who:

➤ *Listens to the concerns, ideas and suggestions of Community members.*
➤ *Listens for conflicts between individuals or organizations.*
➤ *Listens to hear of innovative ideas.*
➤ *Listens to spot trends, to notice common patterns of behavior and to observe the Community mood.*

After bringing what has been heard and observed to the attention of the Community Council for discussion and decision, The Listener Convener will convene whatever meeting seems appropriate to share that information, address those concerns and support the ideas and suggestions that could help move the community forward in its aims. These meetings might be brief discussions of a few interested people or gatherings of the whole Community to address issues that affect them all. They might be to raise awareness, to resolve conflict or to contribute towards the development of the Community.

The Listener Convener also initiates or supports the development of Community projects and activities.

The Community members elect the Listener Convener to the post and pay his or her salary from Community membership subscription. The Listener Convener is to be available to, accountable to, and in support of the individual Community members while keeping in mind the needs and aims of the Community as a whole. Also to hold an awareness of the way in which the Community is perceived and the role it plays locally, nationally and internationally.

The supervision

The supervision I received from Joan helped me to keep an overall view in my role, while noticing details. It assisted me to remain neutral when the needs of individuals and those of the Community were at odds. It helped me to think of innovative ways of engaging people and to encouraging increased Community interaction. It was especially useful in helping me to understand and get to grips with what was my 'stuff' - my concern and my responsibilities, and when these belonged to others.

Although I had for much of my time in the role the support of a part time male Listener Convener colleague, the size and scope of the role could sometimes feel overwhelming. Even though I was an experienced coach and could mentor others in making sensible choices and successfully managing their work and their lives, my commitment to the Community and to its enormous potential, occasionally led me to overextending myself or to have unrealistic expectations of situations; especially of my time and energy.

The benefits

Joan helped me to maintain my equilibrium, create and uphold boundaries and manage my time effectively – mostly! She assisted me to recognize and understand behavioral patterns – mine and other people's – and to deal with tricky situations in challenging times.

Without her support I'm not sure how effective I would have been in that role or whether I would have been willing to stand for the second term, during which time so much was achieved and established in the Community.

Joan offered this regular supervision to me as her voluntary contribution to the Community and has continued to do so with successive Listener Conveners.

This is a notable example of how one hour of expertise voluntarily offered every few weeks can have a significant benefit that can ripple out to touch many others way beyond the person being supervised.

> Having someone in the role of Listener Convener could be of great benefit in voluntary organizations that have many members. It could also be a useful role in any local community.

More information on supervision can be gained in the book, Supervision in the Helping Professions. 3rd Edition – 2006 by Peter Hawkins and Robin Shohet and published by Open University Press. Also on the website of the Centre for Supervision and Team Development: www.cstd.co.uk

The book: FINDHORN COMMUNITY FABLES, contains around 100 stories of people's personal experiences, insights and information regarding the Findhorn Community covering over 50 years. This is available from Amazon in paperback and e-book formats and is accessible through our website: www.youmakethedifference.net

Reviews

Regular reviews can be beneficial to the volunteers and to the organization, especially if supervision is not offered and Mutual Support Groups are not a regular activity.

Reviews with volunteers ought to cover more than the usual work-based issues common in employment situations. They could include such things as how well the volunteers feel their time and skills are being utilised? Do they think they could offer more time or feel the need to offer less? Can they see ways in which they might be more efficient or effective? Are they receiving the information, instructions, support they need to carry out their tasks? Are they feeling satisfied with their volunteering experience?

When managing volunteers it is essential to remember that everything about volunteering, for the volunteer, is a matter of choice!

There is more about review processes later in this book.

8

WHY DO VOLUNTEERS LEAVE?

Q

Questions to consider:
1. What are the main reasons for people ceasing their volunteering with any project, group or organization?
2. How can you retain the volunteers you have?
3. What do volunteers need to remain involved in your organization?
4. What systems need to be in place for dealing with concerns, difficulties or conflicts within the group that might result in the loss of volunteers?
5. What methods could be created to regularly show volunteers appreciation of their time, skills, energy and commitment?

Why do people stop volunteering?

What reasons might volunteers have for leaving the service of an organization to which they have committed time, skills and effort, perhaps over a number of years?

It might be because their circumstances have changed. Situations do alter and life has a habit of moving on. Perhaps the focus of their interest has shifted or they no longer have time to spare.

If these factors have remained constant then the reasons for a volunteer's resignation is likely to be found within the project/group/organization itself. I have noticed that, more often than not, resignations result from some difficulty the volunteer has been having with one or more of the people involved; the way things are being managed or maybe with some of the attitudes or behavior of other individuals.

Over the years I have heard of many reasons for the resignation of volunteers from projects that they were previously passionate about. For the most part, these mostly fit under the headings of:

➢ Inadequate or over-controlling styles of management.
➢ Unrealistic or unreasonable expectations.
➢ Attitudes of indifference towards volunteers or a casual or uncaring approach to their wellbeing.
➢ Burnout.
➢ Poor communication.
➢ Unfulfilled personal needs

Style of Management

Inadequate management

This means either that it is unclear who is in charge of what, or that those people who are recognized as being in charge are not coping or are making a poor job of it. This might be as a result of lack of skill or lack of confidence.

Over-controlling management

In researching this book I came across a resignation letter from a volunteer that succinctly sums up the potential outcomes of an over-controlling management attitude of community projects and groups. I am familiar with the writer and know her to be a very capable and reliable woman dedicated to her community and willing to engage in activities that she believes would have beneficial outcomes.

Part of her letter is published with her permission and with names and places changed.

Resignation letter from Moira:

As several of you already know I decided some weeks ago to resign from our TT (Transition Town) altogether. I stayed on a while longer to complete one of the applications.

I joined the Transition Town Movement three years ago because it embodied my philosophy regarding the environment, community and education. I looked forward to volunteering a few hours a week to something to which I felt drawn.

So why am I resigning?

Well, I could say because of old age and decrepitude and I'm sure you have all seen the signs!

I could say it's about time I started to pay more attention to my health, and that would be true.

I could say I am suffering from acute volunteer fatigue and that is most certainly true! Those few hours turned into 20-30 on a regular basis.

But there is another major reason why I am leaving this TT.

Initially Carol's (Leader of the initiative) energy and commitment enthused me considerably, but I found that both Board and Steering Group meetings were tense. I put this down to the old adage of 'forming, storming, norming and performing'. This particular group of people didn't get past the 'storming' stage and by mid 2009 the 'steering group' had, quite rightly, been disbanded and there were only four people left on the Board of Directors and no project leaders. At this point only one of the major TT projects had begun.

Fortunately, at the next AGM, this position was improved considerably and voluntary project leaders were appointed and work on other projects was begun, although with only 2yrs of the grant to run. The Project Leaders also formed the management committee and although this held together until the projects were completed on time and even a little under budget, they 'performed' without really moving past the 'storming' stage. Much of this arises from a style of management, which may have been appropriate in the business world for some time, but not in a volunteer community group.

The concept of Transition Towns is to engage the community to become more resilient and solve problems that arise in their lives – this calls for a bottom up approach, which is flexible enough to accept other people's wisdom and experience. The Transition Towns movement does not posit any 'right' answers to all situations.

I know that Carol has not been happy with the way our TT has been going for some time, but I am unclear why. Is there a 'correct' way forward? And who is to say which way that is? Can the 'leader' always have the right answer? The top down approach to management that she seems to favor has put ever increasing demands on a very small group of hard working people and has led to frustration, anger, mistrust and games-playing with which I am very uncomfortable and can no longer accept.

I am often put in mind of the Major riding over the hill on his charger looking for new battles whilst the troops are left behind fighting the last one, floundering in the mire and the trenches, undermanned and under resourced. When they do finally catch up, having successfully won the battle, they are court-martialed for not obeying orders!

Yours…etc.
Moira

It is self-evident that a management style that disempowers or frustrates volunteers is unlikely to create a happy band of mutually supportive people in long-term commitment to any project. It seems to me that a project management style that recognizes that the greatest assets in a project are the wisdom, experience and skills of those involved, uses them wisely and with respect, is likely to retain the commitment of those involved.

> A group leadership style that encourages participation in discussion, strategic planning and decision-making by all members of the initiative is likely to result in those people being more fully engaged and willing to bring to fruition the strategies that they had a hand in creating.

Unrealistic or unreasonable expectations

People might resign because they are no longer enjoying their volunteer activities or feeling fulfilled by them. It could be that, in regard to the organization, they are feeling any one, or maybe all, of the 3-Ds:

1. Disappointed
2. Disillusioned
3. Dispirited

These feelings might be about the work they are doing, with the organization through which they are doing it or with their own performance and achievements. In many cases this could be as a result of unrealistic or unreasonable expectations – theirs or other people's.

Expectations of the work

The work might be more difficult than they imagined or less rewarding than they had hoped.

Options:

a. It could be useful to help volunteers to think about the work they are engaged in and to consider whether it is, with the benefit of experience, the best fit for their skills and interests.

b. On the other hand, together you may find that there are several ways in which to make improvements that would lead to their greater satisfaction from their volunteering.

Expectation of themselves

Volunteers might be experiencing disappointment in themselves. Perhaps in how well they are doing with their volunteering, how much they are achieving or even if they are making any difference at all with their efforts.

It could be beneficial for volunteers to be more realistic about what they expect of themselves and others. It is my experience that when expectations are unrealistically high then at least one of the 3-Ds is inevitable.

If volunteers realize that their expectations of themselves are unrealistically high then this could provide them with the opportunity to develop their attitudes of self-acceptance, tolerance and compassion. Recognizing that we are all doing the best we can, and that if we could do better we would, might help them to find some peace of mind and a more relaxed attitude to themselves and to others. That does not mean that they cannot look for ways in which to make improvements.

Expectations of the organization

Organizations that proclaim strong principles and high values will attract individuals with those same principles and values. If these individuals discover that organizations do not live up to their stated principles and values then the 3-D's are likely to set in. Or these may occur when the values of the organization and the individual are at odds with one another.

Some time spent together in examining the reality of the principles and values of the organization, compared to those of the volunteer might clarify the situation for both of you.

You might need to help volunteers to re-adjust their levels of expectation. To assist them to be aware that if their expectations are unrealistically high they might never find an organization to meet them. Moving from group to group in search of the one that will fulfill their ideals could prove to be fruitless and deeply disillusioning for them.

On the other hand, if your project consistently loses volunteers you might usefully look at how well your group is living up to its ethics and values. You could also become more aware of how your expectation of volunteers might be affecting them.

> If your expectations of volunteers are unreasonably high you may never find volunteers to meet them.

In my experience it is rare for the people supporting a project to be happy to put in the same grueling hours of work or have the same high levels of dedication and commitment to a project as the person who launched or leads it.

Burnout

In my experience one of the main reasons that volunteering stops working for people is because of burnout. This is particularly prevalent in areas of volunteering that require sustained effort or continued commitment.

Any individual in any role can experience burnout. However, it seems to be most frequently experienced by people who care deeply about what they're doing, about those they are helping or the project or the organization with which they are working.

> Burnout is common among people who volunteer to care for others or whose work could be of great benefit to people. Burnout is often accompanied by resentment.

Attachment

From years of working with volunteers it seems to me that burnout might be mostly attributed to feelings of attachment.

This could be the attachment of a volunteer to always being reliable and not letting anyone down.

It might be a volunteer's attachment to delivering care and support to those who need it despite difficult or seemingly impossible circumstances.

It could be a volunteer's attachment to the success of a project or to their personal achievements within it.

A volunteer's burnout might be the outcome of their attempts to achieve the results to which the organization or individuals within the organization are deeply attached.

Fiona

Fiona, one of my Personal Culture clients, was the founder and leader of a community project that was floundering. During sessions with me she recognized that she was attached to everything in the project working perfectly all the time; to all the goals being met on time and on budget; to everything that was attempted being achieved 100% and to no approach for help being declined. She was also attached to the project having a good reputation and was attached to herself, her colleagues and volunteers being recognized as being efficient and professional in all situations.

These high standards might be admirable and certainly preferable to laziness, inefficiency and ineffectiveness. However, these standards need to be realistic, which, in Fiona's case, due to lack of funds and personnel, they were not. Because of this they were taking a toll on the wellbeing and the morale of the volunteers. From the way things were going it seemed possible that Fiona's attachments might actually cause the project to fail.

As a result of spending time identifying and reducing some of her attachment to unrealistically high standards and expectations, Fiona was able to release herself and others from some of these stress-producing attachments.

Good enough is good enough

A group of committed volunteers is one of the most powerful forces on the face of the Earth.

For such a group, achieving the difficult seems easy, although the impossible may take just a little longer! Even so, there are times when reality must prevail. That the continuation of commitment is often reliant upon any good efforts made being acknowledged as good enough.

Volunteer's efforts are good enough when they do their work to the best of their ability without exhausting themselves; when they use their time as efficiently as possible without becoming stressed; when they and the organization are realistic and honest about what can be achieved within a timescale and when people do not expect the impossible from themselves or from other people.

I believe that when we can acknowledge that we do our best and that what we do is good enough, we release ourselves, and others, from the tyranny of attachment to perfection.

You can make the difference in your organization when you help everyone involved in it to realize there are times when good enough really means just that!

Poor Communications

Poor communications within any project, group or organization can, and often do, create problems and cause difficulties.

Poor communications can result in inadequate instruction and poorly delivered directions and in these being misheard or the implications not fully understood. However, it is often the subtle aspects of poor communication that can do the most damage in situations requiring trust and cooperation.

Poor quality of listening can leave people feeling unheard. If these feelings are a result of people showing disrespect and lack of attention when they are supposed to be listening this can lead to a sense of disempowerment in those attempting to be heard. When such a situation is extreme in a group the feelings of frustration, anger and resentment created in volunteers often results in their leaving that group.

> Among the aspects of poor spoken communication are shouting, offensive language, insulting or detrimental remarks, judgmental statements, unfair and/or unnecessary criticism and unkind gossip.

Any of these will undermine morale, trust and co-operation within a group.

It is worth remembering that when one or more of these are consistent in the culture of an organization it is unlikely that self-respecting volunteers will remain involved for very long.

Unfulfilled wishes and needs

We have already considered some of the wishes and needs that can be met through volunteering. If people are unhappy in their volunteering it might be because their own wishes or needs are not being met through these activities. If people have not examined their wishes and needs when deciding upon their volunteering role then they may have inadvertently chosen to do something that does not meet those wishes or even something that increases their needs rather than meets them.

Re-evaluating needs

People's wishes or needs may have changed since they first considered volunteering with your group. It could be that their original needs have been so well met through their activities with you that they are no longer a need. It could be useful for your volunteers to take some time to consider the wishes and needs they now have that could be fulfilled through another type of volunteering. If they discover that the volunteering they are currently engaged in is unlikely to meet these new needs, they could then look for another activity or role within your organization that might. If they fail to find it in your project they may feel the need to find it in another.

Time

If people are realizing how much they have to do and how little time they have to do it in, then the timing of their volunteering activities is probably out of balance.

In reassessing time factors, people might come to a number of interesting realizations:

1. They did not have as much time available as they thought they had.
2. Their circumstances might have changed and, instead of being

realistic about the amount of time they now have, they may be becoming stressed through trying to do the same amount of work in less time.

3. In their willingness to be supportive some volunteers might be feeling obliged to put in more hours than they originally intended.

4. Their good nature might be being taken advantage of when they are asked to do more than they had originally agreed to do.

5. They may have difficulty in saying no.

6. They might be overwhelmed if there has been an unrealistic estimation on how long tasks take to complete.

7. Unnecessary or over-complicated procedures might be proving to be extremely time consuming.

8. Cumbersome systems might be leading to inefficiency and so to volunteer's lack of satisfaction in their work.

9. Inadequate training might be resulting in volunteer's feelings of ineffectiveness or their sense of their time being wasted or not appropriately utilised.

Any of these can lead to volunteers feeling stressed. Life can be stressful enough without volunteering activities adding to the pressures people might be already experiencing.

> A reassessment of the amount of time that your volunteers have available for volunteering, how they are using it and the amount of time that tasks actually take, can be helpful to them and everybody concerned.

6. Indifference and lack of respect towards volunteers

Over many years, colleagues and I have experienced numerous occasions when people needing help have sought support in mentoring, coaching or even counseling as a result of concerns and distress they experienced in their volunteer activities. Many more of these kinds of situations have come to light during the research for this book.

➢ We have listened to people as they describe their frustrations in having their expertise undervalued, used inadequately or criticized by the organizations they were voluntarily assisting.

➢ We have heard people describe being left to their own devices in discovering how to work within the systems and culture of an organization and how to find the most appropriate ways of being useful.

➢ We have listened to people talking about the lack of necessary information, instruction, training, equipment and support to really be effective in their volunteering.

➢ We have heard people describe their feelings of inadequacy and disempowerment resulting from harsh criticism from people overseeing their voluntary work.

➢ We have listened to people expressing their bewilderment and disappointment in the attitudes and behavior shown towards them by staff members of organizations, especially when some of those people were themselves volunteers who could be expected to have more understanding of what volunteers need in order to be effective.

➢ We have heard people talk of their concerns and disillusionment in how resources were being used or the way in which an organization's work was being, or sometimes not being, carried out. Occasionally, these same people received responses from the organization indicating that any expression of concern would be considered to be disloyal behavior and an undermining of the organization.

These sorts of occurrences are difficult enough for volunteers to cope with when experienced in their local community. Imagine the effect they have on volunteers who have travelled distances to offer their services, especially when this has entailed travelling from other countries or even continents. We have come across people who have relocated to other countries in order to volunteer with an organization whose work they felt passionate about only to feel indifferently or disrespectfully treated by that organization.

An over-estimated sense of importance

It is interesting to observe how often people have sought our help when volunteering in organizations and institutions whose work could be considered to be extremely important, even vital, to some aspect of life on the planet.

We have noticed that this sense of importance can create an attitude of superiority or self-righteousness in organizations or in some individuals within them. This can lead to a lack of respect for their volunteers and inadequate attention being paid to their wellbeing. There appears to be a belief held within some of these organizations that the importance of their work overrides any needs that their volunteers might have and justifies anything the organization requires of them. There seems to be an assumption that the passion and dedication of their volunteers will keep them committed to the cause regardless of how they are treated.

Within some of these institutions and organizations there seems to be an expectation that there will be a never-ending supply of willing volunteers available to them.

It is our experience, gained over many years and in many parts of the world, that some of these attitudes are surprisingly prevalent in religious and spiritually-based institutions and organizations, whether these are traditional religious institutions or those expounding ancient philosophies or new philosophies for sustainable living.

We have observed that in some organizations dedicated to spiritual development there is no guarantee that the individuals or leaders within them have also achieved high levels of personal development or people skills. We have encountered people, even those ordained or highly respected for their spirituality, whose attitude to volunteers has been described by the volunteers as deplorable.

Not 'bad people'

Those people whose behavior volunteers have described in this way are not usually bad or horrible people. Apart from a few exceptions, these are usually individuals who care deeply about the people, the creatures, the environment or the situations they are trying to help, protect or preserve. These are people who are passionate and fully committed to bringing about results that could change or improve lives or situations.

It is often because of this passion, care and commitment that people find themselves in charge of, managing or coordinating, voluntary workers. They may be attempting to do this in difficult circumstances and with inadequate resources. However, most significantly, they might not be sufficiently skilled in people-management or in interpersonal communications.

> While feeling overwhelmed by the size of the task in hand or the situation facing them, some people can slip into a form of indifference towards, or feelings of detachment from, the needs of those around them who have come to help.

A western manager of a spiritual education Centre in India was heard to say, 'I've got more to deal with than worrying about how volunteers are doing, how they are coping and how they're feeling. That's their problem and I don't want to know. If they can't stand the heat they should get out of the kitchen!'

This attitude is perhaps understandable in crisis situations, in emergencies or when lives are at risk. (Even so, introduction to protocols, clear directions and encouragement ought to be the least amount of support any volunteer might expect.) In long-term projects and every day volunteering activities this type of attitude to volunteers is unacceptable. It is disrespectful to and unappreciative of the volunteers and could rebound detrimentally on the organization and lead to its reduced sustainability.

While people like this manager deserve to be appreciated for their passion and commitment to their project it would be wise to redeploy them to a role where they are not required to deal with volunteers. For the benefit of the volunteers, the organization and the work being carried out it is essential that people responsible for volunteer's working arrangements, support and wellbeing have good skills in interpersonal communications and in managing people.

I have been involved with organizations where there is an assumption that it is inevitable that most, if not all, volunteers will eventually leave. This might explain any attitudes of casualness, lack of commitment and even some indifference towards volunteers from people in these organizations. However, it might be these attitudes that are the reasons for volunteers leaving!

While many instances described in this section as being the reasons why people cease volunteering with an organization might seem extreme they may be more common, at least to some degree, than might be imagined. Whilst it is inevitable that for any number of reasons volunteers will leave a project, a group or an organization, it would be a sad waste of time, effort and resources if this were due to the indifference or negligence of them by other people in those organizations.

Remember: Paying attention to and implementing some of the suggestions for supporting volunteers, will go a long way to demonstrating to people that their choice to volunteer with your organization is still the appropriate one.

> You can make the difference by asking questions within your organization about the volunteers' experiences. This might reveal areas of disquiet or discontent that could to be addressed in order to keep the volunteers you already have.

Make a note

Make a note of more ways in which your volunteers could be supported to stay volunteering with your group, project or organization.

-

-

-

-

-

-

-

-

-

-

-

-

-

-

-

-

-

9

KEEPING YOUR VOLUNTEERS

What efforts are made in your organization to deal with those niggles, gripes, difficulties, complaints and conflicts that can affect the morale of volunteers?

Is any time and attention spent on this or is there a feeling within the organization that volunteers come and go and for every one that leaves there are others waiting to take their place?

Even in the best-run projects, groups and organizations, things happen, sometimes small, seemingly insignificant things, that if not attended to can undermine volunteers' commitment. Sometimes a group or an organization is so busy getting on with the work, coping with insufficient funding or lack of staff or volunteers, that not enough time, if any, is devoted to morale or dealing with those small things that irritate or upset people and make work or working relationships difficult. This can create problems, because, to use a couple of clichés: 'most people tend not to suffer in silence,' and, 'misery loves company.'

Gripes and complaints can become the basis for a groundswell of discontent, disillusion and negative thinking.

This can undermine the effectiveness of the group or project, turn working relationships sour and can create an atmosphere that nobody wants to be in.

Remember: Attitudes within a group or an organization can become tarnished by unresolved small concerns and niggling complaints. It would be wise to devote time to giving these a regular airing and finding solutions to them.

Spring Cleaning

The Spring Cleaning process is effective for dealing with niggles, complaints and gripes as it begins with a Brainstorming session to reveal these problems. Although Brainstorming is usually seen as a way of generating positive ideas, it can also be a useful way to get out into the open all the things that are not working well or those that people in a group feel unhappy about. Because it's not always easy to recognize who is saying what in a Brainstorming session it allows for a certain amount of anonymity and safety for people to say the things they may not feel able to openly express in other circumstances.

I have named this process Spring Cleaning because it is not only an effective way to clean up stuff getting in the way of effective working, it is a beneficial way of starting a new year in the life of a group or an organization. This could be the calendar year or following after the annual general meeting.

This Spring Cleaning process is metaphorically throwing open the doors and windows of the daily workings of the organization, sweeping out the dust of accumulated grumbles, putting the shine back on individual and group attitudes and freshening up the air of mutual support and cooperation.

> A simple version of this process can be held at any time when it is noticed that small issues are building up or when the harmony of the group is out of whack.

Facilitation

This is a process that could benefit from being handled by an outside facilitator. This will allow everyone in a group to participate equally and for departmental heads or leaders of teams in larger organizations to be in the process rather than managing it.

If facilitation is handled from within the group, a main facilitator could manage the process, a co-facilitator could pay attention to the morale and wellbeing of the group and a third person could do the scribing. This will share the load and the responsibility and allow each of those people time to also participate in the process.

Naming the event

It is important that as many people in the project as possible attend this event. This might be achieved by having a title such as, **'How can we improve?'** Along with a subtitle such as, **'Your opportunity to have all your concerns heard'.** It can be surprising how many people who may not normally attend meetings with any enthusiasm might flock to this one!

Inclusive meetings

Make sure that as many of the appropriate people as possible attend. If this process is conducted within a very large organization it could be run separately in each department. Any organization-wide issues arising could then be brought to another meeting of representatives of these departments.

Remember to ensure there is proper representation of every department in order to bring all necessary perspectives to that meeting.

Stating the intention

Begin with a clear statement of the intention of the Spring Clean. Something like: 'We intend to bring into the open for discussion and resolution those large and small issues that are getting in the way of this being a happy, cooperative and effective organization'.

Breaking the ice and creating the atmosphere

Have some activities, preferably fun ones that can help to break the ice, reconnect people with one another, improve trust and increase energy levels. Some suitable games are described in the GUIDE TO GROUP GAMES, which is FREE to download at: www.youmakethedifference.net/free-guides.

The Brainstorming

In the Brainstorming process encourage everyone to shout out something that irritates, annoys, disappoints or disempowers him or her in his or her experience of the organization, project or group.

However, be mindful that the objective at this stage is to identify the areas of concern, the things that are not working well, rather than individual behavior. There is a need to be very clear that this is not an opportunity to put individuals in metaphorical stocks. So no individuals are to be named and no accusations are to be made. If these are shouted out they are not to be written down. The facilitator could ask for a reworded contribution.

If there is some reticence from people, the facilitator could ask some focusing questions. These need to be open questions that require more than 'yes' or 'no' answers. 'What is the… like in the group?' What about the…?' 'What are any of the difficulties with…?' 'What does…?' 'How is…?' There maybe one word answers to some of these questions such as 'terrible, pathetic, poor, inefficient, inconsistent etc.' Each word followed by the area named is written on the board such as 'inconsistent supply ordering'. The facilitator can ask for more concerns about this issue to add to the list.

People can become quite enthusiastic about this process. They may start to shout out things that they've never mentioned before. It is not uncommon for people to shout out witty remarks. This is useful because laughter releases tension and there is usually a grain of truth in most humor. The remark is written on the list like everything else. It may need further investigation or it can be discarded later in the process.

Clustering items

Some items are probably already grouped together on the list. These and other similar items can now be clustered into common themes. The question might need to be asked 'how can some of these items be grouped together?' Or 'what common thread binds some of these items together?'

These clusters could be written on a Mind Map around a hub expressing the purpose of the event, for example, 'How can we improve?' Each cluster is given a heading such as Communication. This cluster would include all the things to do with communication within or put out by the organization. Other cluster headings could be: management, decision-making, resources, lack of volunteers or support, office use, group morale or the reputation of the organization.

This is the stage where the basis for many of the concerns begins to emerge. For example, if the organization is seriously under-funded then that might be the likely cause of people feeling stressed, overworked, frustrated or ineffective.

If the leader or the main managers of the project have poor communication skills then this is likely to have a knock-on effect throughout the organization.

Ranking

Having all the gripes and complaints listed and clustered, people then rank them in terms of greatest concern. Ranking and prioritizing is not necessarily the same thing. An issue that is ranked as of prime concern may not, for many reasons, be prioritized as the first item to be dealt with.

> Note: There may not be any clear ranking due to the fact that people might experience different things from one another and so have differing concerns. This ought to be seen as interesting information rather than a problem.

Prioritizing

Prioritize each of the ranked clusters in order of being dealt with or in terms of urgency to be addressed. The focusing question for this process will need to take into account what is going on in the organization or group at this time. For example, if there is a serious problem with funding or resources, the focusing question might be something like 'how will we prioritize these to take into account our financial difficulties?'

If there is a critical shortfall in volunteers or volunteers are threatening to leave because of low morale, the question might be 'what priority shall we give to these that could improve our volunteer situation? Or 'How shall we prioritize these that will have the most benefit to group moral?'

When the issues have been prioritized the group can then decide when, where and how best to deal with them all.

Next Steps

There are a number of options for these next steps:

Option 1

The rest of the time is spent dealing with each of the issues in turn. If the group is small then everyone can be involved in discussing each item. In larger organizations, small groups could discuss separate issues and bring their findings or suggestions back to the whole meeting. Proposals can be made and voted upon. In my experience this is often the best option.

Benefits

Successfully dealing with all the issues in one meeting can give a sense of achievement and a feeling of empowerment to the group. This can allow people to then implement the decisions made about these issues and then get on with their work.

Challenges

This might be a lot to try to achieve in one meeting and will be dependent on the number of issues identified, the size and seriousness of some of them, the timescale remaining for the meeting and whether or not the people who make decisions (about the budget for example) are present.

If the organization is large there might be lots of small or large concerns that need to be addressed. If a group is new to this process the members might approach it with some casualness. In both cases insufficient time might have been allocated for this process. It is unlikely that the first time any group undertakes a Spring Cleaning it will be completed in an hour or so.

A building in which dust and grime have been allowed to build up and gone unnoticed or unattended to for years will require some time and concentrated effort to scrub and polish it until it shines once more. Items and mechanisms that have broken due to misuse or fallen into decay through lack of use will need to be repaired or replaced. The Spring Cleaning process will achieve this for organizations only if enough time is allowed for it to be completed.

In my experience at least an evening or half a day ought to be allowed for this process. In larger organizations it might take a full day. I am aware that when money is tight or the amount of the organization's work feels overwhelming it might seem to some people to be a waste of time, energy and resources to devote such a large amount of time to a seemingly self-indulgent or even frivolous process. This process is not frivolous, self-indulgent or a waste of time or resources. It can be enormously beneficial for the ongoing effectiveness of organizations and might prevent the demise of small groups and projects.

> Spring Cleaning could be part of an internal conference of an organization or the focus of an away day or a retreat for a small group.

If the appropriate amount of time cannot be allocated for completion of the whole process at one time, the following options could be considered as alternatives. If the process has not been given sufficient time then one of these options will be inevitable.

Option 2

The meeting is adjourned at this point having scheduled a further meeting to deal with each of the issues in order of priority. People may feel satisfied that the processes undertaken have cleared the air and brought issues out into the open. They may feel complete with this part of the process and eagerly anticipate the future scheduled meeting.

Make sure this takes place, and soon!

Option 3

The meeting deals with one of the issues raised. This could be the issue that was given priority or one which people feel confident can be fully dealt with in the time remaining. The group then reschedules a further meeting to deal with the other issues in order of priority. If the issue chosen is fully resolved, this can give people a sense of satisfaction and achievement and raise in them an eager anticipation of the future scheduled meeting. Make sure this soon takes place!

Option 4

The meeting deals with as many as possible of the short, easily manageable items and then schedules a further meeting to deal with the larger issues. Finding workable solutions to a number of niggling items can raise energy levels and create a sense of accomplishment within the group and lead to an excited anticipation of the remaining scheduled meeting. Make sure… you've guessed it!

Option 5

The meeting uses the time remaining to set up working groups, each one with a remit to investigate and consider a different issue. These groups will report back to a whole group meeting on a specified future date. Their suggested options or recommended solutions will be considered and decided upon at that meeting. This can help people to feel that due care and attention is being paid to their concerns, especially if most, preferably all, the people at the meeting will be engaged in one of these working groups.

Challenges

The biggest challenge to all of the options, except option 1, is that some people may not be able to attend future meetings. Also be aware that not having their concerns addressed immediately might leave some people feeling incomplete and frustrated. This could compound any belief they might have that to attempt changes within the organization is futile. Others might feel concerned that issues are being sidestepped or avoided. Indeed, unless these are dealt with in the very near future, they may be right!

Commitment

If the chosen option means delay in resolving issues, it is vital that any commitments for dealing with them are scrupulously kept. Further ongoing meetings are to be scheduled at specific dates and times in the very near future and nothing must happen to prevent them from taking place. Unless these commitments are made and kept, the morale and the attitudes within the organization are not likely to improve. In fact, any promises and commitments broken are likely to result in a further decline in morale and effectiveness.

Preventative procedures

Once this process has been completed for the first time, simple procedures for addressing concerns and complaints ought to be created and implemented by the group - just as regular cleaning will keep any building clean, healthy and functioning properly.

Although an Annual Spring Cleaning may still be a good idea, having a system for regularly identifying and clearing up concerns, complaints and difficulties will prevent a build-up of problems.

The Little things

Some of the small items raised in a review can be quickly dealt with and can result in beneficial changes.

> Having a group sort out small, niggling issues can promote feelings of empowerment and frees up energy for more important things.

It is surprising how much of a difference can be made to people's attitudes when concerns are dealt with in this way. Here are few solutions to small concerns that I have observed to make a difference:

- ➤ Changing the delivery of supplies from once a month to every two weeks.
- ➤ New volunteers being mentored or 'buddied up' with experienced workers.
- ➤ Changing from a Rota system regarding washing dishes that is not working to an agreement for everybody being responsible for washing up his or her own mug and plate after breaks.
- ➤ Delaying starting times by 15 minutes to fit with a new bus schedule.
- ➤ A short Check-In at the beginning of meetings and before the start of work to reconnect everyone and reignite the energy of the group.
- ➤ Creating a newsletter or a bulletin board, real or virtual, to keep volunteers in the information loop.
- ➤ Having small ways for letting volunteers know that their efforts are appreciated.

Make a note

Make a note of new procedures that could be implemented to enable your volunteers to express concerns or complaints.

-

-

-

-

-

-

-

-

-

-

-

-

-

-

-

-

-

Appreciation

As already mentioned, there is a commonly held belief that service is its own reward and that people ought not to seek recognition or appreciation for volunteering their time, effort and skills. In my experience, any group or organization that operates under this illusion is likely to have some less than enthusiastic volunteers who may not stay around for very long. Those who stay may be doing so out of loyalty to colleagues or a deep commitment to a cause. Any advantage taken of these people will ultimately tarnish even the most laudable of goals.

Remember: volunteers might not stay long with an organization where they feel unappreciated.

> A few words of encouragement, acknowledgment of difficulties tackled and appreciation of work well done may be all that is needed to give volunteers the heart to continue.

The less control people have over the decisions that affect their work, the more appreciation they are likely to need in order to stay committed and enthusiastically involved.

> You can make the difference in your project by encouraging the development of a culture of appreciation.

Small appreciations

A nod of acknowledgment or a word of thanks for things done well, on time or with good humor will let people know that their daily efforts are noticed and appreciated. This is not just something for leaders to do. Everyone in a group could contribute to an appreciative culture by behaving this way with one another.

However, leaders can make a regular contribution by taking time in meetings and discussions to acknowledge and appreciate work done well.

Specific Appreciations

Appreciation and praise ought to be as specific as possible.

Telling someone they are 'great' does not really tell them much about what is so great about them or what they are doing. It is often a hollow or meaningless form of praise.

The point to appreciation is letting people know what you have noticed and have valued about them and their work. Be specific about what, how, where and when people did what you are appreciating. Taking a little more time to notice these things might also help you to recognize the value of those who volunteer with you.

Examples of expressing specific appreciation are:

> 'Thank you for…' 'I appreciate the way you…'
> 'I can see how much you have…'
> 'This will help me to…' 'I am grateful to for you for finishing this so quickly. It gives me plenty of time to put this information into the document.'

Knowing what they do well helps people to do more of it and to feel good about themselves.

Immediate Appreciation

Praise and appreciation ought to be given as soon as possible after the action or event.

A delay that separates the appreciation from the action might make it less meaningful. Saving the praising of someone until a major meeting is likely to have less beneficial effect on that person if in the meantime he or she has been feeling unappreciated. Do both! Tell the person immediately and then express the same appreciation in the later meeting.

Authentic Appreciation

I have noticed a tendency towards the use of over-exaggeration in praise and appreciation such as Wow! Fantastic! Fabulous! Etc. Far from expressing a depth of appreciation, these words have lost much of their power from over use.

The same goes for the use of jargon. The fashion in the use of descriptive words probably changes more rapidly than in any other aspect of communication. Most age groups and common interest groups tend to invent their own language. This includes the language of appreciation.

Cool! Awesome! Wicked! These are examples of words that have been in and out of fashion during recent years. Using this kind of jargon is meaningless to anyone outside that particular culture. Doing so when the words are out of fashion, are not valued by the person you are praising, or are not your usual way of speaking, may make you appear false.

Direct Appreciation

Praise the person to their face.

Letting someone know that you appreciate them by telling other people and hoping that the message will somehow reach that person will dilute that appreciation and make it less effective. Do both! Tell the person and then tell others as well.

Small tokens

Small tokens of appreciation can mean a lot. Birthday cards and cakes, Christmas cards or small token gifts on those occasions are nice gestures. There could be annual events where every volunteer is named and shown public acknowledgement in some way. Other forms of celebration, such as being taken out for afternoon tea or some other treat are simple ways of showing appreciation and rewarding the dedication of volunteers.

Simple, authentic, immediate, direct and specific appreciation of those around you will work wonders on so many levels.

When appreciation is at the core of a group's culture then the members of that group are likely to be supportive of one another and be willing to go the extra mile.

Make a note

Make a note of new ways in which your volunteers could be shown more appreciation for the work they do.

-

-

-

-

-

-

-

-

-

Encouraging long term volunteering

I have been involved with organizations whose volunteers are more of a permanent fixture than some staff members. Some people have volunteered with these organizations for years, even decades, and some of them are the second or even third generation of volunteers from the same families in such activities as volunteer lifesaving services.

> Volunteers are likely to feel more committed when they consider the organization, group or project to be 'theirs'.

From my observations and experiences, most people will remain committed to volunteering with a project, group or organization when one or more of the following circumstances exist:

a. They feel a sense of ownership of the group, project or organization and a sense of responsibility for it.

b. They continue to believe in the aims they are supporting.

c. They feel fully included and believe they play a significant part.

d. They see that what they offer is wisely used.

e. They feel they are being effective and that what they are doing is making a difference.

f. They enjoy what they're doing.

g. Their volunteering feels rewarding and fulfilling.

h. Their volunteering makes an improvement in or some contribution to their own lives.

i. They feel respected by the others in the group and those engaged in the project.

j. They feel appreciated for the time, skills, experience and effort they voluntarily give.

You can make the difference to your project, your group or your organization by ensuring that your volunteers experience as many of these criteria as possible.

That is empowering volunteer management!

10

MEASUREMENT, EVALUATION, REFLECTION, REVIEW AND FEEDBACK

Regardless of how often people volunteer with an organization; the size of the role they carry or how significant that role is, they are likely to stay committed when they feel certain that they are an important part of that organization, group or project. This commitment can be even greater when people feel they are making a regular contribution to the sustainability of the organization, group or project.

Measurement, evaluation, reflection review and feedback are essential to ensure sustainability. To make sure that a project is achieving its desired objectives; that the systems, procedures and processes are being appropriately effective, that volunteers are able to carry our their tasks to the satisfaction of everyone, including themselves, and that people in receipt of the organization's work are benefiting from it and are happy with what they are receiving.

It is wise to remember that inevitably things will go wrong from time to time. The trick is to notice when this is happening, investigate what is going wrong and to immediately take action to put things right.

Often the cause for things to stop functioning in the way envisioned is lack of funding, although by no means always.

Beware of throwing more money at a problem that could better be solved by some careful consideration.

Measurement and Evaluation

If your project, group or organization were intended to bring about a change, to make a difference to people or to a situation, it would be wise to consider the following questions:

Q

1. How will you know how effective you are being?
2. How will you establish what effect your project is having on raising awareness or if thoughts and opinions have been changed by your efforts?
3. How will you measure progress and success?

Measuring progress isn't always a high priority at the start of a project. However, creating simple and straightforward ways of gathering data will not only help with monitoring and measuring progress, it can be included in funding applications or used to encourage support.

It would be wise to keep a record of all the project's activities and events.

Options:
a. You could record the number of people who were involved in projects and what the outcomes were.
b. Project working groups could be asked to record information that emerges from their work.
c. It could also be interesting and useful to make a photographic record of activities and progress.
d. To avoid wasting time and resources it would be sensible to have ways for monitoring results of trainings and on the introduction of new systems or processes to check for their effectiveness. This could be achieved through surveys and by requesting and recording feedback from those involved.

Make a note

Make a note of new methods that could be implemented for measurement and evaluation within your group, project or organization.

-

-

-

-

-

-

-

-

-

-

-

-

-

-

-

-

-

Reflection and Review

In all the activities involved in keeping a project moving forward and doing interesting and exciting things, it is easy to forget to ask if the project is moving in the right direction and in a supportive and functional way.

Having regular times to reflect and to ask 'How are we doing?' is an essential safety check.

Opportunities for reflection and reviews can be held regularly for the group to monitor the progress of the project as well as for staff and volunteers to review their personal work, achievements and satisfaction.

Reflection and review upon progress

Regular opportunities for reflection and review on progress, of working practices, systems and procedures will help a group to remain effective and relevant. These are useful when those in the project need to make an assessment of their achievements and progress.

Q

Questions could be asked such as:

a. How on track are we with our objectives?
b. Name some of the achievements that have furthered the aims of the group/projects purpose.
c. How effective is the process on…?
d. What is the most important achievement since the last review/meeting?
e. What has worked well?
f. What has not worked so well?
g. What could be done differently in the future and what new or different steps could be taken?

Volunteers can reflect upon and review their personal work and contribution to the project through these and similar questions. Reviews provide opportunities for people to acknowledge one another for work well done and for efforts made.

The number of questions in a review will depend upon the circumstances and the number of people present. In a small meeting each person present can answer these questions in one Go-Round. In larger events, these could be considered in small groups.

> As well as a way of evaluating work, progress and interactions, a few minutes could be provided at the end of meetings, activities, discussions and decisions to discuss how effective were the processes for these or how they could be improved upon.

Reflection and review on objective, values and ethics

Reflection and review would be useful for assessing in what ways the objectives are being met and how the agreed Values and Ethics are influencing the behavior and working practices of individuals and of the outcomes of activities.

When things go wrong in projects it may be because some people have got their wires crossed about the objectives of that project. The values and ethics of some the staff and volunteers might be at odds with those stated for the project.

Consider some of the following questions:

Q

1. Are the aims and objective that volunteers have 'signed up to' being pursued?
2. Does it seem that the project is veering away from what people believe to be the objectives and towards something that they are not committed to?
3. Are the stated Values and Ethics of the project being adhered to?
4. Are these still compatible with those of the individuals involved?
5. Has something in the project changed since those involved felt inspired to become part of it?
6. Has something in them changed since they joined the project?

It would be worth remembering that working together to identify the answers and deal with the responses to these questions could alleviate current problems and save time and effort later down the track.

Reflection and review on interactions and working relationships

In my experience, dissatisfaction with the work, uncomfortable working relationships, dysfunctional systems, lack of comprehension of how staff and volunteers need to be supported and managed, and little understanding of the development of groups and their culture are the reasons why many projects fail, why volunteers leave an organization or stop volunteering altogether.

One of the challenges of working in projects is that they tend to be full of other people!

The staff and volunteers in projects are often made up of people from very different backgrounds and who have different approaches to life and ways of working from one another.

> Whatever activities people engage in they bring their whole selves to them. They bring their personality, their characteristics, their patterns of behavior, the pain of their past and the hopes for their future. This hope for the future may be the very reason some people volunteer in a particular project

A wage packet or the prospect of promotion might compensate for difficulties with colleagues or managers that can arise in paid employment. What compensation is there for volunteers for putting up with difficulties with colleagues?

Often, the common ground shared by all, the concern, the cause, the reason for people to choose to work in or to volunteer their time to a project, is enough to hold them together and to work out differences or difficulties. Sometimes, this is not enough!

If there are relationship problems between volunteering colleagues, or/and employed staff in an organization it could be worthwhile dealing immediately with those problems rather than risk the loss of valuable people. This will provide people with opportunities for personal development.

Difficulties between people are rarely all one sided, although they may seem that way from each person's perspective! Using conflict or disharmony as an opportunity for self-exploration can be very rewarding.

Sometimes the people with whom we have the most difficulty turn out to offer us our biggest opportunities for self-awareness and self-improvement.

Choosing not to examine the part we might each play in an uncomfortable relationship could be a lost opportunity to know ourselves better. Believing that everybody else is at fault is likely to be an illusion. Any unresolved situation that could cause a volunteer to leave a project might very well reappear in any future project they choose to join.

A reflection and review would be useful for assessing the quality of interactions between people and in what ways these are affecting the activities and outcomes of the project.

Q

This review would enquire into:

a. What has been the most enjoyable aspect of working together?
b. What has been difficult?
c. How constructive are communications between us all?
d. What is one thing that needs more attention paying to it while working together?

To create items for discussion a single word could be asked that would describe areas for review. These could be such things as: communication, co-operation, resources, or timing. Review any relevant items under each heading.

Reflection and review on volunteering

> Having capable and willing volunteers is obviously essential to all Voluntary projects, groups or organizations. It might be vital to the survival of some of them.

If people feel unfulfilled, dissatisfied or irritated with their volunteer work then perhaps they haven't found the right fit. They might be a square peg in a round hole or some expectations, theirs or other peoples, may have been too high. It may also be because they feel underused and undervalued.

Remember: Volunteering ought to be fulfilling. Even though some of the work may be tedious, tiring, challenging, occasionally uncomfortable and sometimes downright dirty, there needs to be some sense of achievement at the end of it.

There might be occasions when volunteering does not seem to be working well within a project for one or all of the following reasons:

➢ Some of the volunteer's hearts may no longer be in the project.
➢ Some of the volunteers might not be adequately trained or managed.
➢ Some of the volunteers could be square pegs in round holes.
➢ Some of the volunteers may have unrealistically high expectations

of themselves; of others or of the role they are playing.

➢ There may be people who have unrealistic expectations of some of the volunteers.

➢ Some of the volunteer's skills might be being underused or undervalued.

It would be beneficial to spend some time reflecting upon and reviewing the current volunteering situation through the perspective of each of these points. Helping volunteers in checking their current experience against what they set out to achieve with their volunteering and what they hoped to receive from it would be a beneficial thing to do.

Q

This review could consider questions such as:
   a. How well are volunteers fitted to their roles or tasks?
   b. Is their training adequate?
   c. Are their skills being appreciated and appropriately used?
   d. How well are volunteers being supported to do their work?
   e. What do they need to become even more effective?
   f. Are people feeling fulfilled through volunteering in this project?
   g. What do they require or need to happen for them to feel so?

Reflection and review on next steps

Having reflected and reviewed all these aspects of the project, it would be wise to identify the next steps to be taken to deal with or improve these situations and to move the project forward in the most appropriate ways.

Q

Questions:
   1. What steps could be taken to move forward with what has been identified?
   2. What will you/we do differently from now on?
   3. What changes will you/we now make as a result of what we have learned?
   4. What contribution will you/we now make towards fulfilling the agreements that have come out of this review?
   5. How will you/we recognize when those changes have been made?

These sorts of questions can bring further clarity and may provide an obvious forward direction. They can assist in reinforcing key elements of a reviewed issue and can encourage commitment to action.

Review processes and many more useful questions for a variety of situations are among the processes described in the books ENJOYABLE AND EFFECTIVE MEETINGS and EFFORTLESS FACILITATION in the YOU MAKE THE DIFFERENCE series available in paperback and e-book formats from Amazon and accessible through our website: www.youmakethedifference.net.

On Track Review

Projects can lose momentum and become ineffective when the people in them or managing them do not pay enough attention to keeping aligned with the purpose and objectives. When those involved do not recognize or admit to one another that they are off course for achieving the goals and objectives of the project, this might result in loss of support from volunteers and from elsewhere. The On Track Review is useful for checking these out.

After the current reality has been honestly recognized then work can be done on identifying what the ideal situation might be and how to get from what currently exists to the on track ideal in the most effective and mutually supportive manner.

Applications
This process is useful in a number of situations:
1. If the project seems to be off track.
2. To review progress at the end of the year or some other significant period.
3. In preparation for the Annual General meeting.
4. When a project seems to be losing effectiveness.
5. When a project is in some kind of difficulty.
6. As a preparation for an application for major funding.
7. When an organization is making a significant change such as applying for charitable status.

If a large number of people participate, this process can be conducted in common interest groups such as departments within an organization or the stakeholder groups who would be affected by the outcome.

Outside facilitation
This could be an event that would benefit from outside facilitation. If that is not possible then several group members working together could facilitate it.

On-track Review process

Step 1. Starting the process

The purpose and aims of the organization, group or project as currently stated are written up on a board or flip chart that is visible to everyone. This might reveal that some people involved have not been completely clear about the purpose of the project or the aims of the group. In rare cases this could show that the purpose and aims have never been clearly defined, in which case some work will obviously need to be done on that before moving to step 2.

Step 2. Visualization

Working alone, each participant visualizes the best setup they can imagine to fulfill the project's purpose as stated. Visualizing the Ideal Day within the organization or project is an effective process to use for this.

The participants write down everything they would want to happen during an ideal day in the organization, group or project in order to be on track to achieve its stated objectives. They are to put in every exquisite detail they can think of in the areas posed by the following questions:

Q

1. What activities would be engaged in?
2. Who would be engaged in them?
3. Where would these activities take place?
4. What facilities, equipment, resources and support would ideally be available for these activities?
5. How would it feel to work in these circumstances?
6. What would be the ideal outcome of these activities?
7. Anything else?

These questions are to be addressed by each person as the Ideal Day is described by them as though it is a diary of the events throughout one day. Starting with the moment of approach the building or first task of the day and ending when there is nothing else to be done on that day.

This process can help to widen thinking. For this reason, I would recommend that in their imaginations, people would consider there to be no restrictions of time or money in the creation of their Ideal Day.

> If it can be imagined, it can happen in this Ideal Day.

Does someone want to have a bigger and better equipped building to work in? No problem, they simply visualize how such a building would look. Do they want to have a famous film star launch a new project? Easy, they just imagine that person doing so. People are to be encouraged to allow their imaginations to go as wild as possible.

> This is not the time for limited thinking or self-censorship. Some of the more outlandish ideas can be used as metaphors later in the process. If people tell themselves something is silly or not possible, they ought to write it down anyway.

Everything is written about in glowing, positive terms: the sights, sounds and smells, the colors, the atmosphere and the attitudes of the people.

AVK
There are reasons for being aware of the sights, sounds, smells and colors when visualizing an Ideal Day. We are each usually predominately Auditory, Visual or Kinesthetic in our mode of learning and experiencing. The use of each of the senses while creating the Ideal Day will help to make the visualized activities stronger and more memorable, regardless through which of those modes each person best receives information.

It is especially important to remember this when taking groups of people through this exercise because they are each likely to have their imaginations triggered differently from one another.

Remembering that the aim is to identify the ideal circumstances through which the project or organization could achieve its goals, each imaginary Ideal Day is to be full, rich, interesting, exciting and joy filled. If it is not like that, it needs to be re-thought.

From experience, I recommend that participants are encouraged to keep writing from the start, regardless of what comes into their minds, rather than spending time pondering or getting their thoughts in some order. A useful trick is to keep the pen point on the paper. This seems to help to keep thoughts flowing.

Step 3. Sharing the day
The group or groups now reform for everyone to take a turn in reading out their Ideal Day to everyone else in their group. Each Ideal Day description is to be listened to with respect and encouragement. It is important that no derisory remarks or negative comments are made by any of the listeners. The contents of each person's Ideal Day are indications of

the dreams that this person has for the potential of the organization, group or project. Not only that, many of these descriptions will be used as metaphors and symbols for what could be made possible.

> At the end of each person's story their contribution is to be applauded by everyone in the group with delighted enthusiasm and appreciation.

A synopsis of what is said is written up on a board, although no names of who said them are indicated.

Step 4. Sharing the Common Ground

Through a process to identify common ideals through linking similar ideas and grouping related ideals together, a picture will emerge of the ideal circumstances for continuing to carry out the objectives of the organization, group or project.

This is also the time to consider the metaphors and symbols represented by some of the ideals. Most of the seemingly unrealistic ideas can be seen as metaphors or symbols for changes that could be realized. For example, a lavish party at the end of the day could represent a need for more celebrations, social interaction or perhaps to feel more valued and appreciated. The dream of going to Paris for lunch might indicate a desire for some mutual leisure engagements or perhaps more adventurous food in the cafeteria. The more outlandish ideals like sending food planes to Africa and having stars to open projects might indicate a need for more direct action or ambitious thinking.

Step 5. What already exists?

Now that people have identified their Perfect Day in which their ideals for achieving the organization, group or project's purpose are identified, it is the time to look at what currently exists.

Working alone once more each person recalls an actual day in the life of the group, project etc. that they experienced some time in the recent past. It is useful if the day chosen has some aspects to it that were of concern or that did not turn out so well. To obtain the widest possible snapshot of the life of the group etc., it is important for each person to choose their own specific day, not one dictated by the facilitator.

Everyone writes down all the details of the happenings of their chosen day exactly in the way they experienced it. As with the Ideal Day, this is written down in diary form and every actual detail is recorded, including the outcomes of any decisions and actions and the feelings that the person experienced.

> This part of the process is about being realistic, not creative.

It is intended to bring out into the open what really happens on a day to day basis and what already works and what don't work so well in fulfilling the organization, group or project's purpose.

Remember that it is imperative that all information is included. That opinions and thoughts about what works and what do not work well are based upon people's experience. This is a good way to remember the things that work well in the organization, the things to be proud of. This is an opportunity to be realistic about what doesn't work so well in the project, things to be less proud of.

> Although it is vital for people to be honest, it is not about blaming the system or shaming any individuals.

It is not about bemoaning the lack of funding or railing against an unjust world. It is about identifying and recording the details of what actually happens day to day.

To prevent it from becoming a depressing or chastening exercise, the facilitator manages this in a light manner. Perhaps lightening the mood by bringing gentle humor in where appropriate.

Step 6. Sharing the reality

As before, everyone then shares with one another what she or he has written down. This is a vital part of the process that allows everyone to hear and acknowledge what really goes on from personal experience rather than from the perspective of gossip, or rumor.

It might be uncomfortable for some people to speak about or to hear things that might be considered negative. Even so, it is vital to do so. If the pitfalls in previous thinking, current initiatives or ideas for potential projects are not identified, then whatever problems or dysfunctional systems or behavior that already exist in the organization, group or project, are likely to be perpetuated. This is the ideal time and process for the recognition of those potential pitfalls to come to light.

As before, a synopsis is written on a board. Common themes will probably appear as the areas of related experiences are linked. Others can now be explored.

Step 7. Getting from here to there

By now, how close to or how far from being on track for the project achieving the highest ideal objectives will have become clear. Perhaps the gap is encouragingly small. Maybe it is alarmingly wide. The areas that require work will have become apparent.

It is time to consider how to get from where the organization, group or project currently is, to where it now clearly and ideally would wish to be. The questions to ask are:

Q

1. How on track are we?
2. Which parts of the shared ideal are already in place?
3. What parts of the current reality need to be improved?
4. Ought any of these to be discarded altogether?
5. How to fill in the remaining gaps?
6. What new and revolutionary ideas identified in the ideals can be initiated to move us forward to a new and more ideal way of being on track?
7. How can we do that simply and mutually supportively?

> This is the time for participants to inspire and empower each other.

Step 8. Working groups

After identifying these ideas, working groups can now be set up to pursue them. If this is a full day event then this work, or at least some of it, can be carried out immediately; otherwise future meetings will need to be set up. A careful record ought to be kept of who will do what and by when and how these will be reported back to all those who have participated in this event.

> Note: It is important that everyone involved in the process so far is included or suitably represented in these ongoing discussions and decisions to prevent feelings of exclusion and any potential for undermining or sabotaging the outcomes.

Ending process

A suitable ending process such as a Go-Round will allow participants to share their thoughts and feelings about the event with everyone in the group or in their new working group. If time is short then a Paired Sharing will give them the opportunity to share with at least one other person.

Closing

The facilitator sums up the process, reiterates the decisions taken, clarifies the work to be done in the working groups and announces the date of the next follow on meeting at which the working groups will report progress.

Appreciations all round. Close.

Make a note

Make a note of new opportunities that could be implemented within your organization for regular review and reflection.

-

-

-

-

-

-

-

-

-

-

-

-

Feedback

> Feedback is an important source of information. It enables people in a project, group or organization to learn firsthand about its effectiveness or otherwise and to discover what is working well and what is not.

Receiving feedback

There are two ways of receiving feedback - directly and indirectly.

Indirect feedback

This is delivered gradually over time as people don't carry out their roles effectively, there is discontent and disharmony within the group, people leave and projects fail.

> This kind of feedback is inevitable if issues are ignored in the vain hope of avoiding criticism and conflict or facing problems that might be difficult to deal with.

By putting off or avoiding dealing with difficulties; in not setting up simple means for those involved to give direct and regular feedback to management or to one another, people in projects can create the very situations that they are trying to avoid.

The antidote to this is to have regular opportunities for direct feedback built into the culture of the group and project.

Feedback questionnaires

A common practice is for the use of questionnaires for review and evaluation and especially as methods for receiving feedback. This written form may be a requirement by those to whom the group is accountable or to be used as a way to follow-up on decisions and actions. It can be useful to have a practice run to trial questionnaires to ensure that they make sense and really will provide the key information required.

Sometimes questionnaires require no signature and so some people might use this anonymity for making criticism or expressing opinions that they do not have to stand behind or explain to anyone. While this is a way to receive information that might not otherwise be forthcoming this seems to be less than desirable in community projects and mutually supportive groups. I think this creates a lost opportunity for people to take responsibility for what they say and for all those involved to hear perspectives that may be similar to or quite different from their own.

On one occasion I observed feedback questionnaires being collected at the end of an event and then dumped straight into the waste bin!

> There is absolutely no point in producing questionnaires if there is no intention of using them. In fact, if the people who have taken the trouble to fill out questionnaires come to realize that their feedback has been ignored, they are likely to become upset, angry or resentful.

Because questionnaires need to be written, reproduced, handed out, collected in, read, recorded and probably filed away, in some circumstances, such as having small numbers of personnel available, they might be more trouble than they are worth.

Complaints

> Many people fear complaints because they think they are indications of failure. And yet, in most cases, complaints are valuable feedback.

People who complain are offering very clear feedback about something they are unhappy with. Complaints from or about volunteers are opportunities rather than problems, unless they are unheard, ignored or not remedied.

Obviously, it would be better if there is no cause for complaint in the first place and of course there are people for whom complaining seems to be a way of life. In these cases complaints may emerge as grumble or gossip. Even so, there is maturity and wisdom in seeing complaints as opportunities to improve working practices and offer better service.

> You could make the difference by helping those you work with to turn any of their complaints into direct feedback that can be clearly received and appropriately acted upon.

Direct feedback

Direct feedback is when the volunteers involved in a project are able to express concerns, talk about progress of how things are working or not, and what they are thinking and feeling about things directly with one another and the people who can do something about the relevant situations. This feedback is a gift to be appreciated!

11

LETTING GO

There will be occasions when you will feel it necessary to ask people to cease volunteering with your project, your group or organization. The reasons for this may be due to some aspect of their work, their behavior, their attitude, their level of skill or something that makes it inappropriate for them to remain involved.

Whatever the reason for it, the conversation to cease their involvement ought not to come as a surprise to them or to you. Previous conversations, meetings, feedback sessions, Mutual Support Groups, supervision and various methods of clear communication ought to have provided ample opportunities to bring whatever the difficulty is out into the open for discussion regarding remedial action or improvement.

> With the best will in the world, it is not always possible to support people to behave more appropriately, or to improve their skills, behavior and attitudes sufficiently for them to remain an active member of a particular volunteer team.

If your role requires it, it will be up to you to communicate clearly and honestly with a person the reason why it is necessary for them to leave the project or group. In most circumstances this can be done with kindness, even if a person has behaved inappropriately or in some way reprehensibly.

Using the principles of creating and delivering a Complete Feedback Message you will be able to make the situation clear to this person without humiliating them. This type of conversation is not comfortable for either person involved and it may take courage on your part and the need for compassion, both for the person involved and for yourself.

Occasionally, volunteers leave because they are unhappy with something or someone within the organization. If self-disclosure or opportunities for regular feedback are not strong elements within the culture of the group you may not know why a person is ending their volunteering time with you. Some people may of course say that they're leaving for personal reasons when they are not. It may take courage for them to be honest about something that has been upsetting them, especially if they have kept it to themselves or have denied there has been anything they have been unhappy about.

The following type of conversation would give you the opportunity to thank them for the work they have done and offer them the opportunity to talk about what they have found difficult or upsetting. These conversations can be stand-alone or be a part of a final review process.

Completion clearing conversations

These are conversations that allow people to end their involvement in a project with some grace and leave it with a sense of completion for themselves and the others involved. It is not intended to be a last opportunity for a slanging match or for throwing around accusations and unkind criticism.

Remember, completion clearings are always to be conducted in 'I statements'.

Process

As the one who has initiated the conversation you begin by offering some appreciation of the person who is leaving for what they have given to the project. There are bound to be some things to appreciate and it would be helpful for them and for you to have them leave knowing what those are. Make this appreciation specific and detailed. Not only will this let the person know exactly what you have valued, it could encourage them to be equally specific and detailed when giving you their feedback on their experience of working with the organization.

Then, continue by asking if they would like the opportunity to discuss their reasons for leaving. If you do not know the reason, or have doubts about the original reason given, this could provide an opportunity for the person to bring their experience or concerns into the open. It could help this person to talk about the situation, support them to get over it, and, perhaps, to prevent a similar distressing situation from occurring again in your project.

What you hear from them might surprise you. There may have been things going on about which you knew nothing. This could provide an opportunity for further conversation with all those involved. There might be things that need to be remedied or even apologized for. Even at the last-minute a clearing conversation with the person might help them to change their mind and stay involved.

There may be nothing that could have been done to make the situation any more acceptable to that person. On the other hand, it may become clear that they themselves have contributed to the situation or even been the cause of it.

End the completion clearing by saying one more thing that is positive that you appreciate or value about the person who is leaving.

All good things come to an end

Sincere efforts to empower, support and retain volunteers often will result in people happily continuing to offer their volunteer support to projects, groups and organizations for many years. However, many good things do come to an end and volunteering is no exception.

People will choose to cease their volunteering with your organization for all sorts of personal reasons. It is important that they end their involvement with your group feeling their time has been well spent, that they have gained a great deal from the experience, that they have been appreciated for their efforts and that they have made a difference.

Final review

> A final review process can ensure that a volunteer's work has been handed over successfully and that all loose ends have been tied off. It will enable the volunteer to be appreciated for their dedication and contribution to the project.

Whatever the reasons for a person choosing to leave, it can be helpful to the ongoing development of your organization for them to give feedback of their volunteering experience.

There could be a number of areas that you would like feedback on.

These could include specifics such as the quality of the training, support, management, instruction and communication within the organization. There could be wider issues like job satisfaction, working conditions, quality of the service provided and public perception of the project.

It would be useful to remember that people can be more willing to offer feedback on some issues when they are about to leave than they may have felt able to convey while still fully engaged with a group.

In larger organizations this feedback is sometimes obtained through questionnaire or detailed feedback forms. However, it would be courteous to the volunteer and useful to your organization to go through the questionnaire with the person during their final review. This is particularly the case when this is in smaller groups and projects. This might be your last opportunity to benefit from the experience of this volunteer and to appreciate them for their work.

Appreciation Completion

When a long term volunteer or one who has played a significant role in a project is leaving a group, a completion event will give everyone who has worked with or been involved with them the opportunity to show their appreciation and offer good wishes.

This event might take place on the day of the person's leaving or very close to it. An open invitation could be made to include anyone who would care to attend.

These affairs are sometimes managed by a facilitator or some kind of master of ceremonies and could be expected to take around an hour, perhaps a little longer if the group is a large one or if the person has been involved with many people over a long time.

Everyone is seated in a circle so that they can see everyone else. The facilitator asks the person leaving to start the process by speaking about their time with the organization. This can include what their involvement has meant to them, such things as the highs and lows, and, perhaps, an appreciation of the value of the project and of the other people involved.

It is now the turn of those other people to speak appreciatively about that person and their experience of them. In my experience, this appreciation often includes some short anecdotes – touching and/or humorous - that all those present can enjoy. Not everyone will need or perhaps want to say something. However enough time ought to be allowed for most of the people present to speak for a minute or two.

When the facilitator has ascertained that no one else wishes to speak he or she could round up the proceedings by also saying something appreciative. The person leaving might like to be given the opportunity for a brief response to what they have heard.

> If the completion process is not something that is part of the culture of your group you can make the difference to the way people leave it by introducing this process.

Celebrate!

Whenever possible mark the leaving of volunteers with a celebration.

Have a goodbye party, encourage everyone in the group or the team to go out for lunch or, at the very least, arrange for a special cake to arrive during the last tea break of the person who is leaving.

You could provide a card for everybody to sign. This would include everyone who has been involved in the volunteer's activities, including clients and anyone who has benefited from this person's efforts.

A thank you gift might be appropriate too. While individual team members or clients may want to make their own personal offerings, something from the whole group or the organization is likely to have significance for a volunteer, especially one that has been with the organization for a long time.

Whilst flowers and wine are nice to receive, they don't last very long. It could be more meaningful, and provide a volunteer with a long-lasting memory, for a gift to be carefully chosen to be appropriate and significant to that person.

Keep the door open

You could make the difference to your project, group or organization and to the volunteers who are leaving by letting them know that they would be welcome back at any time. Whether that's just popping in to say hello to offer occasional volunteer support, or to return as a fully committed member of the team.

> Knowing the door is always open to them can reinforce to volunteers that they have made a difference in the project, group or organization, and that they could do so again anytime they choose.

Make a note

Make a note of the ways in which the leaving of your project, group or organization can be made more supportive for your volunteers.

-

-

-

-

-

-

-

-

-

-

-

-

-

-

-

In Conclusion

The manner in which volunteers are recruited, integrated, trained, supported, managed and encouraged says a great deal about any organization. When all of these are done with mindfulness, sensitivity, responsibility and care, it demonstrates the attitudes and the qualities of empowering volunteer management.

Providing people with the circumstances in which they can feel empowered in their volunteering will make a positive difference to the quality of their volunteering experience. Not only that; by demonstrating these attitudes you will be showing your own qualities and also be indicating that these attitudes and qualities are likely to be found in all other aspects of your project, group or organization, which could be supportive to how it is perceived by others and be beneficial to its ongoing sustainability.

MORE YOU MAKE THE DIFFERENCE BOOKS

Ripples created by our actions inevitably make some difference in the world. These books are intended to encourage and help people who want to make a positive difference to their lives and to the world around them.

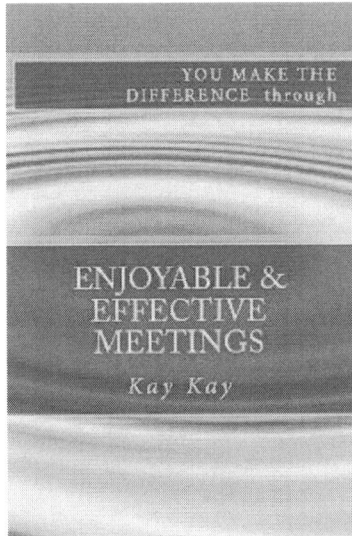

YOU MAKE THE DIFFERENCE
through
ENJOYABLE & EFFECTIVE MEETINGS

Following the guidelines for constructive participation, for efficient chairing and supportive facilitation, adopting the suggested attitudes, implementing the methods, skills, tools, essential procedures and useful processes will guarantee improved effectiveness and enjoyment of any meeting.

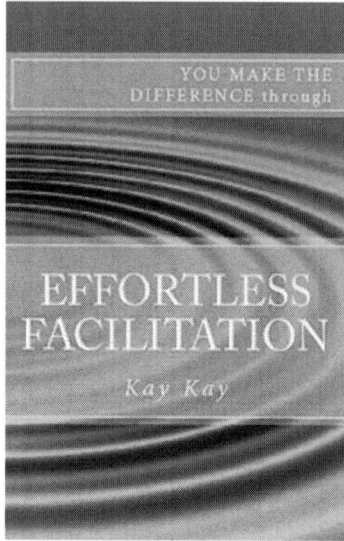

YOU MAKE THE DIFFERENCE
Through
EFFORTLESS FACILITATION

This book is packed with suggestions for planning and designing meetings and events, useful methods and tips for facilitation, empowering and productive processes and a variety of ready-made meeting designs to fit many situations. The implementation of these will guarantee inexperienced facilitators becoming skillful and experienced facilitators becoming even more accomplished – effortlessly!

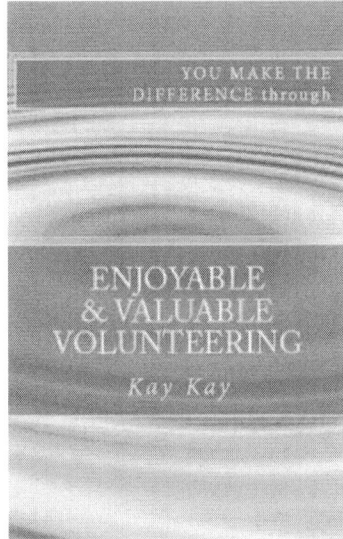

YOU MAKE THE DIFFERENCE
Through
ENJOYABLE & VALUABLE VOLUNTEERING

Ripples created by our actions inevitably make some difference in the world. This book is intended to help people who want to make a positive difference through their volunteering. It contains simple and exciting methods for people to explore what skills and experience they could volunteer, where and how they can easily make their valuable contribution, how to look after themselves while effectively helping others and the many enjoyable ways in which volunteering will enrich their own lives.

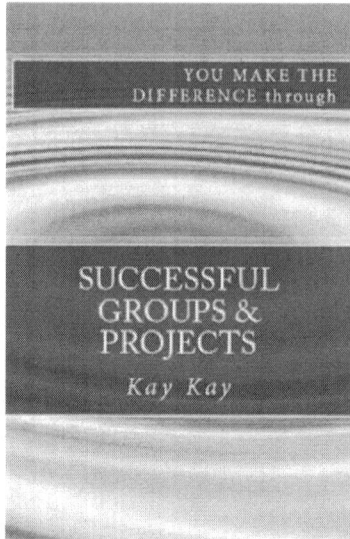

YOU MAKE THE DIFFERENCE
Through
SUCCESSFUL GROUPS & PROJECTS

This book offers insights into how groups work and why they sometimes fail, successful start-up and maintenance of projects that achieve the purpose and objectives, methods for attracting and keeping appropriate members and volunteers. The adoption and implementation of the suggested attitudes, the strategies for obtaining resources, the efficient use of time, money, skills and effort, and the respectful, cooperative ways people can enjoy working together will guarantee success of any group or project.

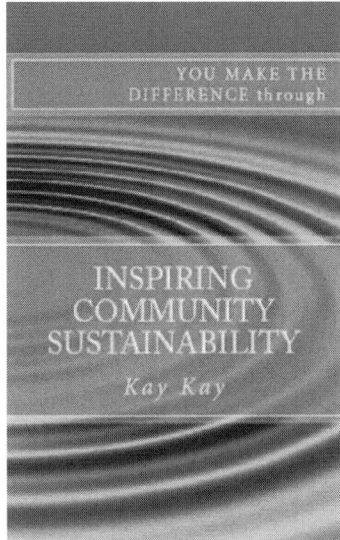

YOU MAKE THE DIFFERENCE
Through
**INSPIRING COMMUNITY
SUSTAINABILITY**

The answer to many of the difficulties facing society is creating a greater sense of community. This book is filled with information and insights, developed through decades of research and experience, on the elements essential for achieving sustainability in any form of community. Utilizing this information, adopting the suggested attitudes, and implementing the recommended systems and processes will guarantee greater sustainability in communities, whether they are rural or urban, traditional or intentional, Transition Towns or Ecovillages.

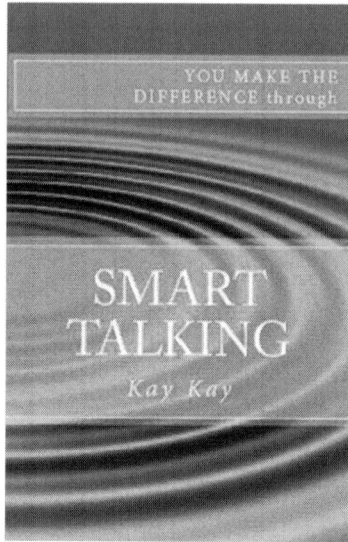

YOU MAKE THE DIFFERENCE
Through
SMART TALKING

Each time we open our mouths to speak we will inevitably have an impact upon those to whom we are talking. This book aims to show the consequences of having a negative impact and offers insightful suggestions for creating a positive effect. Following these guidelines and the suggested attitudes, skills and tools that can relieve stress, enhance relationships and improve communication in so many areas of life will guarantee anyone becoming a Smart Talker.

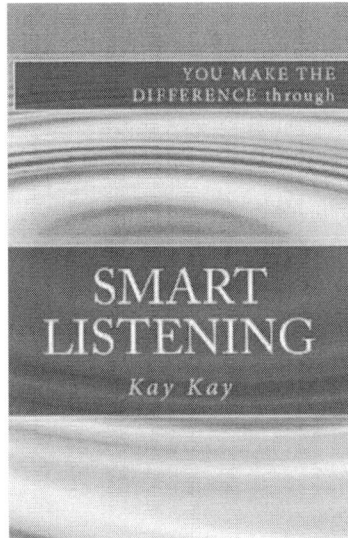

YOU MAKE THE DIFFERENCE
Through
SMART LISTENING

Each of us will inevitably have an impact upon the individuals to whom we listen that is either positive and beneficial or negative and potentially damaging to individuals and society. Implementing the attitudes, listening skills, tools and techniques suggested in this book will guarantee a positive effect that will greatly improve personal and working relationships, reduce conflict, enhance many areas of life and be supportive to people's confidence and self-esteem.

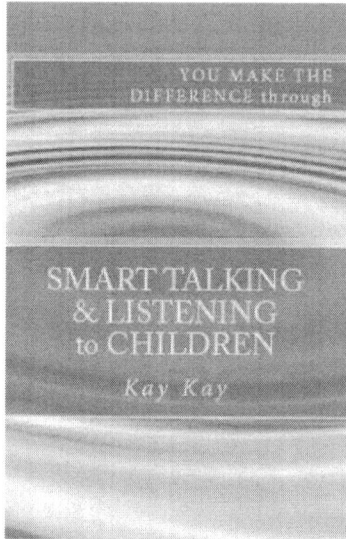

YOU MAKE THE DIFFERENCE
Through
SMART TALKING
& LISTENING TO CHILDREN

From the moment children are born they are learning to become the adults who will manage the future. What kind of future might adults be influencing through the way they talk and listen to children? This book is crammed with skills, tools, insights and suggestions on how adults can be supportive through their communication to the development of youngsters and contribute towards a safe, sustainable future in the hands of well adjusted, capable, empowered, responsible and caring people.

ABOUT
YOU MAKE THE DIFFERENCE

Tim and Kay Kay, the two generations of cultural creatives who founded YOU MAKE THE DIFFERENCE, believe that it is now essential for people to behave supportively with another, to become more engaged in their local community and to cooperate and work together for a sustainable future. The books and website are intended to encourage and support people to achieve the positive difference they wish to make in their lives and in the world around them.

To help with this, Kay Kay, the author, offers decades of experience gained in a variety of professions and cultures, and shares her practical philosophy, knowledge, skills and insights into beneficial ways of behaving, working and communicating with one another and contributing to society.

Tim, as collaborator, book designer, publisher and Webmaster, brings his creativity as an artist and writer, his in-depth knowledge of Buddhist philosophy and the skills and considerable experience gained through living, working and studying in many countries.

All the YOU MAKE THE DIFFERENCE books are intended to be enjoyable to read and easy to use - by everyone. The wealth of information is concisely written to be of benefit to professionals wishing to upgrade their skills; busy people working to make a difference in their communities and at the grassroots of their societies, and people from different cultures, especially those from the developing world, for whom English may be a 2nd or even 3rd language.

On the website: www.youmakethedifference.net there is more background information; GUIDES on a variety of interesting and useful subjects that are FREE to download and the opportunity for people to become part of the Global YOU MAKE THE DIFFERENCE network.

"We each make a difference in the world every moment through our words, actions and behavior, whether we are aware of it or not. The trick to being a smart human being is to choose to make a positive difference."

Kay Kay

11683180R00091

Printed in Great Britain
by Amazon.co.uk, Ltd.,
Marston Gate.